Mark, Matthew and Luke as You've Never Seen Them Before:

A Theoretical History of the Writing of the Synoptic Gospels

Ray Dykes

Mark, Matthew and Luke as You've Never Seen Them Before:
A Theoretical History of the Writing of the Synoptic Gospels

Published in 2006 by Pair o' Docs Press,
9205 Lansbrook Lane
Oklahoma City, Oklahoma 73132

Library of Congress Control Number: 2006936496
ISBN - 0-9723884-2-7

Acknowledgments

This book is dedicated to the intellectually honest people of
First Presbyterian Church of Norman, Oklahoma,
who participated in a Sunday School class on this subject
in the winter and spring of 2006, and especially to
Marty and Tamara Cain and Gary Rife and Jonella Frank
who provided the financial underwriting for the class.

I owe a debt of gratitude to my two New Testament professors
at Vanderbilt Divinity School, Leander Keck and Robert Funk,
for their vastly different approaches to New Testament studies
and for their inspiration to do creative thinking.

Thanks to my wife, Donna Stokes Dykes,
for her careful editing

Thanks to my son, Dave Dykes,
for his excellent work with cover design and book layout

Notes on the Cover:

Cover illustrations represent the gospels.

Luke is symbolized by the winged ox.

Matthew is symbolized by the winged angel.

The winged lion symbolizes Mark.

The foundation symbol represents Paul, who was the apostle to the earliest Christians outside of Jerusalem

All symbols referred to in the text as four-tiered wedding cake.

Contents

Introduction

Nobody, including this author, knows for certain who wrote the Synoptic Gospels, where they were written or when they were written. I was taught in Baptist Sunday School that Mark was written by John Mark, who was Simon Peter's little helper; that Matthew was written by Matthew, a.k.a Levi, who was a tax collector in Capernaum and one of Jesus' twelve disciples; and that Luke was written by Paul's physician friend and companion. It was implied that these three men wrote their accounts of the life and ministry of Jesus just as quickly as they could after his death and resurrection so they could remember his every action and very words.

Little did I know that in the outside world of scholarship, outside of a Baptist Sunday School class, scholars had been speculating for a few hundred years that this just wasn't so. There were questions raised about whether any one or all three of the supposed authors could even read and write. There were considerations about the implications of the variant quality of the Greek in which the gospels were written. Some scholars said this gospel was written in one place and other scholars said the same gospel was written elsewhere. Yet, in the past few years I have had conversations with two Presbyterian New Testament scholars who still hold that Mark, Matthew and Luke penned these gospels. One of these men said I was an "enemy of Christianity" just to speculate otherwise.

Nevertheless, since nobody knows for certain the details of the authorship, what I was taught in Baptist Sunday School is a theory, not a fact. It is a statement of faith. This book contains another theory, a theoretical history of the writing of these three gospels. It is, I believe, a legitimate theory based on internal evidence found in the gospels themselves. We do not have any external sources to which we might go to verify and validate

11

this or any other theory about the writing of the Synoptics. Therefore, I contend that there is information in the gospels themselves that suggests who wrote them, where they were written and when they were written.

One important feature of this theory is that these three gospels stack up like a four-tiered wedding cake. Paul's beliefs and teachings about Jesus form the bottom layer. He is foundational to all the Synoptic Gospels. Mark is the second layer, directly incorporating Paul's theology into the first story written about Jesus' ministry. Matthew is the third layer, using almost all of Mark to constitute 60% of that gospel and then adding 40% new material. Luke is the fourth layer, taking almost all of Mark for 60%, adding another 20% from Matthew and creating 20% new material. The scribes of both Matthew and Luke put their spin on Mark.

A second important feature is that each of these gospels presents a different concept of the humanity and/or divinity of Jesus, a different concept of the mission and purpose of Jesus and a different concept of God's realm. Even though they have so many words and phrases and events in common, the gospels reflect the differences of the communities in which they were engendered. These differences are substantial and have been glossed over in the past. They tell us that early Christianity was not monolithic in belief. The faith was varied in understandable ways.

A third important feature is a demonstration of how each gospel reflects the conditions on the ground in the church that produced it. The thoughts and feelings, needs and wants of the Christian community in each of these three cities, Rome or Alexandria or Antioch, come through loud and clear in their individual gospels. One values power and needs a savior. Another values knowledge and needs a great teacher. Another values social justice and needs a prophet. One church is made up mostly of slaves, another entirely of Jews and another almost completely of Gentiles (non-Jews).

This book was written for the student of the New Testament. Prior knowledge of some of the content of these gospels is assumed. However, it is hoped and believed that a beginning student of the Bible may be able to glean information here that will be useful when reading Mark, Matthew and Luke in depth for the first time. This is not a scholarly book, full of research notes and footnotes. It is hoped that scholars may get ideas from this theory and follow up with their scholarly research to support or not support it.

There are references to Zoroastrianism and Gnosticism throughout the book and no place to exhume and autopsy the corpses in good fashion. Therefore, the reader is encouraged to seek further information about this religion and philosophy, respectively, in other places. They both were important influences upon the gospel writers and Paul.

I invite you to see what I saw as I looked deeply into these three gospels. I hope it makes sense to you. I hope you see some logicality in this theory. It would have been heresy to my Baptist Sunday School teacher and may be heresy to my presbytery, but I can only claim that it is my theory and is as valid as any other theory, and all we have about the writing of the Synoptic Gospels are unprovable theories.

I am indebted to the Jesus Seminar and Bob Funk for the Scholars Version of the New Testament, which is the translation that forms the basis of the textual quotes from the gospels in this book. I have paraphrased or re-translated many of the passages.

Chapter 1
Paul Establishes the Foundation
for the Synoptic Gospels

His Greco-Roman name was Paulos. His Hebrew name was Saul. He was born in 4 CE in Tarsus of Cilicia, a province in what is today southeast Turkey. His Jewish father had obtained Roman citizenship for himself. Therefore, Paul was also a Roman citizen. He was given a thoroughly Jewish education in Tarsus and was taught the tent-making trade. He was never married and had no children.

He went to Jerusalem to study under the wise Rabbi Gamaliel, a Pharisee in the tradition of Rabbi Hillel, the compassionate branch of Pharisees. He became over-zealous for the Torah in the tradition of Rabbi Shammai, the strict branch of Pharisees. It is possible that Saul was in Jerusalem at a Passover when Jesus was there, but the two never met. He had no first-hand knowledge of the biography of Jesus and in his writings only mentioned events in the last week of Jesus' life.

Saul lived in Jerusalem for a goodly number of years after Jesus' departure. At some point, he began to persecute the followers of Jesus, wherever he could find them. In The Acts of the Apostles, we are told that he was given warrants for the arrest of "people who belonged to the Way" in Damascus of Syria (9:1-2). Traveling on the Damascus Road, he reportedly had an experience that changed him and the future population of the Planet Earth. He himself wrote, "...when God... was pleased to reveal his Son to me, so that I might proclaim him among the Gentiles..." (Galatians 1:15-16). The scribe of Acts wrote that Paul experienced the voice of Jesus, calling to him from the sky, judging him and finding him guilty of persecution and providing forgiveness and the means of salvation (9:3-6). If this story is factual (and I hope it is or Paul's primary theological piece is only a con job), Paul experienced Jesus as one who had returned from Heaven to Earth to judge him. This Damascus Road event was the single most important event in the formation of Paul's theology, and Paul's theology is the backbone of all Christian theology. Paul's hope and faith was that his experience would be repeated soon for the whole of the human race.

As the result of this experience, Paul turned Jesus of Nazareth into "Jesus Christ." (Paul made "Christ" to be Jesus' last name, essentially, even though he knew that "Christos" is the Greek translation of the Hebrew word "Messiah," meaning "anointed one.") The poor stonemason (the Greek word translated by the English as "carpenter" is *techton*, which means "builder" and buildings were made of stone) from a backwater area of Palestine known as Galilee was transformed by Paul into a god, the second-in-command to the Highest God of the whole world. Paul tells us he worked alone for three years in Arabia and/or Damascus (Galatians 1:17-18), not conferring "with any human being," hammering out a new belief system that centered on "Jesus Christ." What he constructed he later wrote in his letters to the churches, and his belief system was so brilliant that it met the needs of so many back then and meets the needs of so many today.

Paul's Letters and Other Letters

There is agreement among scholars that Paul actually wrote seven letters attributed to him. The other six letters are disputed as to Pauline authorship for two reasons: the Greek vocabulary in the six is different from the seven, and the theology in the six is not always consistent with the theology in the seven. Here is the author's best guess as to the dates and authorship of all thirteen letters.

I Thessalonians . . . . .51 . . . . Paul
Galatians . . . . .54 . . . . Paul
I Corinthians . . . . .54 . . . . Paul
II Corinthians. . . . . .55 . . . . Paul
Philippians . . . . .56 . . . . Paul
Romans . . . . .58 . . . . Paul
Philemon . . . . .60 . . . . Paul

Colossians	62	Disciple of Paul
II Thessalonians	62	Disciple of Paul
Ephesians	80	Disciple of Paul
I Timothy	110	Admirer of Paul
II Timothy	110	Admirer of Paul
Titus	110	Admirer of Paul

Colossians and II Thessalonians may have been dictated by Paul to a scribe, a disciple of Paul, who may have taken liberties with the wording and the theology. Paul was beheaded in 64 CE, so the last four letters are the works of disciples and admirers who honored Paul by attributing these letters to him.

There were other letters written that bear Paul's name but were not considered authentic by the early church fathers, including III Corinthians and the Letter to the Laodiceans. The Letter to the Hebrews was believed by Clement and Origen of Alexandria to have been written by Paul, but others disagreed.

From Paul's authentic letters, these are his faith inventions, based on his fervent and genuine hope.

Second Coming of Jesus Christ Tomorrow

Paul introduced his first blockbuster doctrine in the first letter he wrote, the first letter to the Church of Thessalonika, the first "book" written in the New Testament, penned in 51 CE (approx.). It is important to note that all of Paul's letters were written before the first gospel was written. In the tenth verse of the very first chapter of I Thessalonians, he gave his idea of the immediate return of Jesus from heaven:

> "...and to wait for his Son from heaven, whom he raised from the dead – Jesus, who rescues us from the wrath that is coming" (1:10)

and

> "...at the coming of our Lord Jesus with all his saints" (3:13b).

This is the first written expression in the history of the world's religions of (1) a god's return to Earth (2) to judge the human race (3) at the end of time, (4) after a previous sojourn on Earth. None of the other prototypes of Jesus (e.g. Buddha, Mithras, Dionysus, Gnostic Savior) had come back, and only Dionysus was expected to return.

In the fourth chapter of this same letter is Paul's imaginary vision of the second coming of Jesus, based on his Damascus Road experience, which included Jesus in the clouds of heaven, judging him and redeeming him. He hoped and believed this same event would take place for the human race immediately. Paul's eschatology (thinking about the end of the world) is not new, but the piece about Jesus' return to judge humankind tomorrow is new and original. This is a very powerful motivational idea, convincing many of the need to believe in Jesus without hesitation. "This new god means business" is Paul's message. This vision of the second coming is repeated in the first gospel written, the Roman Gospel known as Mark.

> "But we do not want you to be uninformed, brothers and sisters, about those who have died, so that you may not grieve as others do who have no hope. For since we believe that Jesus died and rose again, even so, through Jesus, God will bring with him those who have died. For this we declare to you by the word of the Lord, that we who are alive, who are left until the coming of the Lord, will by no means precede those who have died. For the Lord himself, with a cry of command, with the archangel's call and with the sound of God's trumpet, will descend from heaven, and the dead in the Messiah will rise first. Then we who are alive, who are left, will be caught up in the clouds together with them to meet the Lord in the air; and so we will be with the Lord forever."
> I Thessalonians 4:13-17

Special Status of Martyrs

In this same section (I Thessalonians 4:13-17), Paul speaks to the needs of the community who have lost family members and friends to Roman persecution of the new Christian sect. He tells them that the martyrs will be honored at the second coming by being united with the divine Jesus in the air before those who are still alive. This is a powerful assurance to the families of those martyred and encouragement to face martyrdom bravely.

Doctrine of Substitutionary Atonement
"For God has destined us not for wrath but for obtaining salvation through our Lord Jesus Christ, who died for us, so that whether

we are awake (alive) or asleep (dead) we may live with him."
I Thessalonians 5:9-10

"Grace to you and peace from God our Father and the Lord Jesus the Messiah, who gave himself for our sins to set us free from the present evil age, according to the will of our God and Father..."
Galatians 1:3-4

"And the life I now live in the flesh I live by faith in the Son of God, who loved me and gave himself for me." Galatians 2:20b

"The Messiah redeemed us from the curse of the Torah by becoming a curse for us..." Galatians 3:13

"For our paschal lamb, Christ has been sacrificed."
Corinthians 5:7b

Paul introduced the idea of Substitutionary Atonement at the end of his letter to Thessalonika. He then expanded that idea in his letter to the church in Galatia, his second "book" in the New Testament, written in 54 CE (approx.). Paul's speculation was that Father God sent Son Jesus down from heaven to die, as a substitute for the human race, and to atone as the sacrificial lamb for the sins of the human race. Sins are not acceptable to God. Therefore, the human race would be unacceptable to God at the end of the world, before and until the sacrifice of Jesus. Atonement was an important part of Paul's Jewish heritage because of Yom Kippur, the Day of Atonement. For him, this would have been the most sacred day of the year. The high priest in Jerusalem was presented two goats on this day. He sacrificed one of the goats for the sins of the people. The other goat, the "scapegoat," he turned loose in the wilderness, symbolizing the taking away of the sins of the people. Paul modified and adapted the sacrifice of a goat to atone for the sins of family or community and presented Jesus as "the Lamb of God."

Doctrine of Justification by Faith in Jesus

"...a person is justified not by works of the *Torah* but through faith in Jesus Christ. And we have come to believe in Christ Jesus, so that we might be justified by faith in Christ..." Galatians 2:16

"Now it is evident that no one is justified before God by the *Torah*; for 'The one who is righteous will live by faith.'" Galatians 3:11, quoting Habakkuk 2:4, "...the righteous live by their faith."

To be justified is to be made acceptable for salvation in heaven with Jesus. Paul believed that faith in Jesus, as opposed to following the *Torah*, will make one spotless before Judge Jesus on Judgment Day. What it means to have faith in Jesus is not altogether clear, but it is clear that there are Greek Gnostic elements involved, such as the secret knowledge (gnosis) or wisdom. *"But we speak God's wisdom, secret and hidden…"* I Corinthians 2:7 (More about Gnosticism in later chapters)

Identification with Jesus through Experience

"I have been crucified with the Messiah…"
Galatians 2:19b

"…I carry the marks of Jesus branded on my body."
Galatians 6:17b

A revolutionary concept of knowing a god by sharing the experiences of the god. Paul invented the prototype of what is called "Spiritual Death" or "the dark night of the soul."

Two God System

"Grace to you and peace from God the Father and our Lord Jesus Christ" is the greeting used by Paul in his letters to the churches. Paul thought in terms of a hierarchical system with God and Son of God. "Our Lord Jesus Christ" is a god, yet clearly subordinate to God the Father. Paul was not a Trinitarian, since the Doctrine of the Trinity was not in Paul's Bible and had not yet been invented. The Doctrine of the Trinity is not in the New Testament either. In his benediction of II Corinthians, he used a triadic formula, a group of three, but not a trinitarian formula. Paul is not a monotheist either, defying his Jewish heritage that Yahweh is the only God in existence.

Spirit of God as Divine Spark

The spirit of God or "Holy Spirit" is not the third person of the Trinity for Paul, but the connecting entity between God and humans, originating and emanating from God and an extension of God. There is a mystical element involved here, as Holy Spirit can best be understood as an invisible umbilical cord, extending from God to the divine spark or spirit or soul trapped inside the human body, through which the gifts of God are transported from God to the human, especially to those humans who have faith in Jesus.

Theological Dichotomy

Paul sets up flesh, *Torah* and **slavery** as polar opposites of **spirit, Jesus** and **freedom.** Each of these triads is a unit in Paul's mind. The flesh is sinful and *Torah* makes clear just how sinful flesh is, with the result that humans are slaves to sin. The godly spirit yearns to gain freedom from the flesh, and that is accomplished through faith in Jesus Christ. This dichotomy is expressed throughout his letter to the Romans, written about 58 CE.

Conclusion

The point of this chapter is to say that Paul's influence on the theology of the Roman Gospel of Mark was pervasive. Since the other two Synoptic Gospels were built on the Roman Gospel, it is fair to say that Paul's theology was foundational to Mark, Matthew and Luke. The Alexandrian Gospel of Matthew fought against Paul's divine Jesus for their own important reasons, presented in Chapter 4. The Roman Church (where Mark was written) and the Antiochian Church (where Luke was written) both had the privilege of being taught by Paul himself, and Paul shines through their gospels fairly unabated.

Chapter 2
Mark Is the Pace-Setting Roman Gospel

The Gospel of Mark is the gospel of the "People of the Way" in Rome. "People of the Way" is what the Roman Christians called themselves. It is their corporate expression of faith, written around and between 68 - 70 CE by their best scribe and dedicated to John Mark, the faithful helper of Simon Peter. Some of the stories about Jesus may conceivably have come from John Mark – tradition has it that he made it to Rome with Peter – but the odds are great that Mark himself was illiterate. There are no known copies of this gospel that were made before the middle of the fourth century. The scribe for the People of the Way in Rome was probably a male slave with limited knowledge of Greek. This gospel may have been written first in Latin, then translated into Greek. The text is considered to be penned in fourth-grade Greek.

The Gospel dedicated to Mark may tell us more about the People of the Way in Rome, their needs and hopes, than it tells us about the historical Jesus. Their narrative tells us what they needed Jesus to be, what they needed Jesus to do, and what they needed Jesus to say. Almost certainly, they were heavily influenced by Paul's vision of Jesus as a god and the only son of God who lived in Galilee, died in Jerusalem, returned to Heaven, and who was returning soon at the end of the world to judge the human race, rewarding the faithful and punishing the unfaithful. One can imagine that the People of the Way sent small groups of brave people to the house in which Paul was a prisoner to hear his thoughts about Jesus. Their gospel thus became the second tier of the Synoptic Gospel wedding cake.

The Roman Gospel introduced Jesus as the Son of God. Influenced by Paul's theology, the People of the Way believed Jesus to be totally divine in nature, therefore needing no miracle birth story and no resurrection appearances. Jesus is second-in-command to the Highest God of any people or culture or nation, especially to the God of the Jews, Yahweh.

The Roman community included many miracles in their account of Jesus' ministry to show to those who had eyes to see that God had given power to God's son. It was important to them to say that Jesus was as powerful as any of the other Greek and Roman gods. They hoped with all their hearts that God's empire was coming into existence tomorrow, and that Jesus would return tomorrow as the conquering Emperor of the Empire of God on Earth. "Empire" to the Roman mind is the meaning of two Latin words: *imperium* and *regnum*, the latter sometimes translated as "kingdom." To the Roman mind there were no kingdoms remaining, only one empire.

They also used their reservoir of stories about Jesus, which were over forty years old, to construct their narrative. Some of these stories possibly came from Simon Peter and John Mark, if one or both of them made it to Rome as Catholic tradition contends. Other stories may have come from a variety of sources, including from other philosophies and religions of bygone or then current times.

The Gospel of Rome reflects its environment: physical, historical, demographic, philosophical and theological. In the physical sense, the Romans were great builders. Rome was the most modern city in the world at that time, with many conveniences that were not matched for the next 1,800 years. The Forum and the Circus Maximus were the dominant structures. The Coliseum had not yet been built in 70 CE. There were palaces, temples, aqueducts, splendid homes with running water in pipes, public baths and paved streets which made the city a great place to live. It was almost a privilege to be a slave in such a city.

It is critical to understand the historical facts on the ground when this gospel was written. The Roman Republic became the Roman Empire in 45 BCE with Julius Caesar as its first emperor. After the murder of Caesar in 44 BCE and many battles, Octavian became emperor as Augustus Caesar in 27 BCE. Augustus was succeeded in 14 CE by Tiberius, who was followed by Caligula in 37 CE. Caligula held power for only four years and was followed by Claudius from 41-54 CE.

Then came Nero from 54-68 CE. It was Nero who ruthlessly persecuted the People of the Way, crucifying them and throwing them to the wild beasts in the Circus Maximus. When Nero decided to do some urban renewal in Rome in 64 CE, he had fires started to burn down dilapidated structures. The fires got out of hand and burned more than intended, and "Nero fiddled while Rome burned." He blamed the People of the Way for setting the fires and intensified the persecution. This drove the community further underground into the catacombs when and where they practiced their faith in worship. The tradition says that Paul was beheaded in Rome in 64 CE while Nero was emperor. Under pressure from his military commanders – some of them deduced that he was insane and were on their way back to Rome to kill him – Nero committed suicide in 68 CE. In the year 69 CE there were four different emperors. In 70 CE, the city of Jerusalem, including the Temple, was destroyed by the Romans. The destruction of Jerusalem is reflected in this gospel.

The People of the Way had to assume that chaos had broken out in the Empire, and that the Roman Empire was at the point of collapse. This was the opportunity, spoken of by Paul, for God to institute the Empire of God with Jesus as the Emperor. Until that actually happened, they had to remain underground, the seed growing beneath the surface. They also couldn't give away the secret of Jesus' messiahship, so they wrote in their gospel that Jesus denied that he was the Messiah again and again. The enemy must not get their hands on that information. Therefore, they included the messianic secret motif.

In terms of demographics, Rome had over one million inhabitants at the time the Roman Gospel was written and was the largest city of the Empire. Two-thirds of these people were slaves from all over the empire. Among them were Jews, Greeks, Asians from present-day Turkey, Syrians, Egyptians, Persians, Germans, Gauls (French) and Britons. Even the slaves enjoyed a higher standard of living than most people in the Empire. Latin was the language of Rome, but Greek was still the most common language of the Empire. Jewish slaves were a fairly large minority of the People of the Way. There is no way to know how many people, Jews and Gentiles, constituted the People of the Way in Rome, but it was a goodly number since they had high enough visibility for Nero to blame them for the burning of Rome. There were losses from that number due to Nero's persecution, but were also gains from those who were impressed by the faith of the martyrs and the way the community cared for widows and orphans.

With a few exceptions, the first-century Romans couldn't think their way out of a paper sack, philosophically speaking. The Greeks were brought on board to do philosophical thinking for them, including educating their children. Persian Zoroastrianism and Greek Gnostic thought forms dominated, and the number two was very important. Everything was dualistic: body and soul, heaven and earth, light and dark, etc. Power was the most valuable currency. Most things in Rome were about power, including information.

There were hundreds of gods recognized and worshiped in Rome. Monotheism was not a popular belief in Rome. Many religions were made legal by the Empire, including Judaism, but Christianity (as it was later called) was considered an illegitimate sect of Judaism and therefore illegal. Emperor worship was high on the list of religions. Mithraism, a recognized branch of Zoroastrianism, was a favorite religion among the Roman legionnaires, who worshiped Mithras, a good god who was sent to Earth to teach people how to live moral lives and win battles. Dualistic thought culminated in a division of the gods into good gods and bad gods and usually one good and one bad, as in Zoroastrianism.

Conclusion

There is general agreement among scholars that the Gospel dedicated to Mark was written in Rome. The theory presented in this book says that it was written by a community consisting primarily of slaves from across the Roman Empire, expressing their hope and faith in what could have been their last will and testament. Fortunately for Christianity, some of them survived the persecution and their gospel was spread abroad.

Chapter 3
Content of the Gospel Dedicated to Mark

The Roman Gospel is the shortest of the Synoptic Gospels with only sixteen chapters in English Bibles. In the original text there would have been no indication of chapters and verses. Modern scholars have often noted two important themes in this gospel, namely, the secret messiahship of Jesus and the high number of miracles performed by Jesus. The debate over the longer ending of this gospel (16:9-20) is largely ended, with the conclusion that it was tacked on many years later for reasons that are not clear. The purpose of this chapter is to present an outline of the gospel with notes, in the hope that the reader will follow this with a Bible open to the Gospel dedicated to Mark.

Chapter 1

"The beginning of the good news of Jesus Christ, the Son of God." **The lead sentence reflects Paul's double name for Jesus and Paul's concept of the divinity of Jesus. There is no need of a birth story for a god, so none is offered.**

Quotes from Malachi 3:1 and Isaiah 40:3 – **Indicating that Rome is familiar with the Hebrew Bible, probably in Greek**

Ministry of John the Baptist – **John is important to the People of the Way in Rome because they identify with him in his proclamation and his arrest and martyrdom.**

Baptism of Jesus in which Jesus is claimed by God as God's Son – **Paul's concept of the Two God System, with "God the Father and our Lord Jesus Christ" is reflected in this version of the baptism.**

Temptation of Jesus in wilderness – **Satan is the Persian Zoroastrian divine expert in temptation. The use of this name for the tempter indicates the religious pluralism present in Rome.**

Arrest of John the Baptist – **This is to identify John's arrest with the arrest of People of the Way in Rome at the very beginning of the gospel. Jesus' arrest comes toward the end of the gospel. John announced Jesus when he showed up at the Jordan River. The Roman Church will announce Jesus when he shows up soon in Rome as the Emperor of the Empire of God. They felt a real kinship with John.**

Jesus in Galilee, proclaims that Empire of God is starting immediately – **Paul's Second Coming of Christ and the Roman church's idea of the impending Empire of God are blended here.**

Asks Simon, Andrew, James and John to help him in his ministry

Teaches in synagogue and heals man with "unclean spirit" – **This is first passage in Mark not included in Matthew, but is included in Luke. First of many miracles in this gospel**

Heals Simon's mother-in-law – **The point of all the miracle stories in Mark is to show Jesus' godly power.**

Heals sick and demon-possessed in the evening – **Shows Jesus as powerful as Asclepius, the legendary healer known throughout the Empire**

Prays alone in isolated place – **Not included in Matthew, but is included in Luke**

Preaches and heals throughout Galilee

Heals leper and his reputation spreads

Chapter 2

Teaches in Capernaum and forgives sins of paralytic – **Forgiving sins is a divine activity.**

Debates issue of forgiveness of sins with Pharisees and Sadducees – **As far as the Church in Rome is concerned, the Pharisees and Sadducees were not bad people. They just liked to debate with Jesus.**

Calls himself "Son of Man" and heals paralytic – **The Roman scribe is trying to help Jesus keep his messiahship and divine nature a secret. "Son of Man" or "Son of Adam" can mean "human being."**

Teaches beside Sea of Galilee

Asks Levi to help him in his ministry – **"Levi" becomes "Matthew" in the Gospel dedicated to Matthew.**

Eats with Levi and "wrong crowd" and is criticized by Pharisees

Debates issue of fasting with John's disciples and Pharisees

Debates issue of Sabbath observance

Chapter 3

Debates legality of "doing good" on Sabbath

Heals man with withered hand and infuriates Pharisees

Prepares plan to escape over water from crowds wanting to be healed – **Not included in Matthew, but is included in Luke**

Tells unclean spirits not to give him away as "Son of God" – **Keeping his messiahship and divine nature a secret, because the Roman Church must also keep it a secret to avoid persecution**

Appoints twelve disciples/apostles to preach and cast out demons: Shimon Kephas (Simon Peter), Ya'akov Bar-Zebedee (James, son of Zebedee), Yoannes (John, son of Zebedee), Andreas (Andrew), Philippos (Philip), Bar-Tholomaios (Bartholomew), Matthaios (Matthew), Thomas, Ya'akov Bar-Alphaeus (James, son of Alphaeus), Thaddaios (Thaddeus), Shimon (Simon, the Zealot), and Youdas Yiscarioth (Judas Iscariot) – **These were their names in Aramaic, Hebrew or Greek.**

He is accused of being demon-possessed and debates role of Satan in demon possession.

His mother and brothers and sisters come to take him back to Nazareth and care for him. – **The implications are that Jesus, the Son of God, no longer needs his human family, and further, they don't understand that he is divine.**

Refuses to acknowledge his family and calls disciples his family

Chapter 4

Parable of Sower and Seed – **The Church of Rome identifies with the seed, since they, too, are hidden below the surface in the catacombs for worship, waiting to sprout when Jesus marches into Rome as the conquering emperor of the Empire of God.**

Discourse about Secret of Empire of God – **God's coming Empire has to remain a secret until it happens.**

Explanation of Parable of Sower and Seed – **The other seeds that don't make it underground will die at the hands of the Romans.**

Teaches about passing along what you receive – **Stewardship, evangelism, discipleship**

Parable of Seed Growing Secretly –

"The Empire of God is like this: suppose someone sows seed in the ground, and sleeps and rises night and day, and the seed sprouts and matures, although the sower is unaware of it. The earth produces fruit on its own, first a shoot, then a head, then mature grain on the head. But when the grain ripens, at once the sower sends for the sickle, because it's harvest time."

This is the first of four passages not included in either Matthew or Luke. Again, they are identifying the seed with the underground church of Rome. The churches in Alexandria and Antioch do not identify with the seed, so they don't see the need for this parable.

Parable of Mustard Seed – **A small Roman seed will become something large when the Empire of God is inaugurated.**

Jesus calms storm on Sea of Galilee. – **Like the Greek god Poseidon or the Roman god Neptune, Jesus is a powerful god.**

Chapter 5

Heals Gerasene man who was demon-possessed

Resurrects daughter of Jairus, leader of synagogue – **Only gods can raise people from the dead.**

Heals woman with hemorrhages

Chapter 6

Teaches in synagogue in Nazareth and is rejected

Sends out twelve to preach, cast out unclean spirits and heal

Story of Herod Antipas arresting and killing John the Baptist – **More identification between John and the Roman martyrs**

Apostles return to Jesus and report on their mission – **Not included in Matthew, but is included in Luke**

Teaches and feeds five thousand men – **Plus women and children?**

Disciples get in boat on Sea of Galilee while Jesus remains behind to pray

Jesus walks on water to disciples' boat and calms wind – **More comparison to Poseidon and Neptune**

Boat docks on east side of lake and crowds flock to Jesus.

He heals many.

Chapter 7

Pharisees confront Jesus about violations of food purity laws.

Jesus argues that food is not impure but excretion is impure.

Travels to Tyre and heals daughter of Gentile woman

Travels to Decapolis region and heals deaf man

Chapter 8

Feeds four thousand people

Pharisees ask Jesus for verification of his authority and he declines. – **Keep the secret!**

Jesus and disciples discuss feeding of multitudes.

Restoring sight in Bethsaida –

They arrived at Bethsaida. Some people brought to him a blind man, and pleaded with him to touch him. He took the blind man by the hand and led him out of the village. And he spat into his eyes and placed his hands on him, and he asked him, "Do you see anything?"

When his sight began to come back, the first thing he said was, "I see human figures, but they look like trees walking around."

Then he put his hands over his eyes a second time. And he opened his eyes and his sight was restored, and he saw everything clearly. And he sent him home, saying, "Do not bother to go back to the village!"

He told his disciples to have a boat ready for him on account of the crowd, so they would not mob him. After all, he had cured so many, that all who had diseases were pushing forward to touch him. Whenever the unclean spirits faced him, they would fall down before him and shout out, "You Son of God, you!" But he always warned them not to tell who he was.

This is the second of four passages not included in either Matthew or Luke, and for no apparent reason.

Jesus asks disciples who they say he is.

Peter calls him "Messiah" and Jesus tells disciples not to tell anyone about him. – **Keep the secret!**

Tells disciples about his future death and resurrection – **First passion prediction**

Peter rebukes Jesus, and Jesus calls Peter "Satan." – **For reasons not known, the Roman Gospel gives Peter a harder time than any other gospel, even though the tradition has Peter as the first bishop of the Roman Church.**

Jesus commends martyrdom without shame. – **It is very important for the Romans that Jesus utter these words because of the persecution they are suffering.**

Chapter 9

Jesus says Empire of God will arrive with power before the death of some of those present. – **Here it is! Bingo! This is what the People of the Way need to hear from Jesus!**

Story of Transfiguration -- **Preview of the coronation of Jesus as emperor of Empire of God, with Moses and Elijah on the imperial podium with him**

Jesus tells Peter, James, and John not to talk about Transfiguration until after Resurrection. – **Keep the secret!**

Heals boy with seizures after disciples could not heal him

Tells disciples about his future death and resurrection for the second time

Teaches disciples about greatness and humility

Teaches disciples that "whoever is not against us is for us" – **Not included in Matthew, but is included in Luke**

Teaches about stumbling blocks and the Valley of Hinnom

Chapter 10

Debates with Pharisees over divorce

Blesses little children

Teaches rich man that he only gets to keep what he gives away

Teaches that focus on Empire of God and focus on wealth simultaneously are impossible

Teaches that those who are faithful to him will be given eternal life

Tells disciples about his future death and resurrection for the third time

James and John ask for glory and Jesus denies them.

Jesus teaches other ten disciples that glory is gained by servanthood. – **Remember that the vast majority of the People of the Way were servants/slaves.**

Heals "blind" Bartimaeus – **Can a blind man run straight to Jesus when Jesus is standing in the middle of a crowd?**

Chapter 11

Story of Triumphal Entry into Jerusalem – **The Roman military would never have allowed a triumphal parade into Jerusalem during Passover. What we have here is a preview of Jesus' triumphal entry into Rome as the new Emperor of the Empire of God.**

Jesus curses fig tree.

Physically attacks economic system of Temple

Chief priests think about how to kill Jesus. – **Not included in Matthew, but is included in Luke**

Jesus teaches disciples about prayer.

Debates with chief priests et al. about divine vs. human authority – **How interesting! Clearly, the Roman Church is only interested in Jesus' divine authority.**

Chapter 12

Parable of the Vineyard and the Wicked Tenants

Pharisees try to trick Jesus with question about paying taxes to the Emperor. – **Important issue for a Christian in Rome**

Sadducees debate with Jesus over the resurrection of the dead.

Jesus defines the greatest commandments.

Quotes from Deuteronomy 6:4-5 and Leviticus 19:18

Poses question to Pharisees about the son of David

Quote from Psalm 110:1

Jesus condemns the Pharisees.

Praises the widow for her giving spirit – **Not included in Matthew, but is included in Luke**

Chapter 13

Jesus foretells the destruction of the Temple in Jerusalem. – **Indication that destruction of the Temple was known in Rome before this gospel was finished. This is why many scholars date the writing of the Roman Gospel to 68-70 CE.**

Describes the beginning of the End Time

Foretells the persecution of his followers – **The Church of Rome knows this well.**

Describes the coming of the End Time

Describes the coming of the "Son of Man" – **Another vision of the Emperor Jesus marching into Rome**

Foretells the End Time will happen before this generation passes away – **Reassurance for Roman Christians that the End Time is the End of the Roman Empire**

Advises followers to be ready for the End Time

Chapter 14

Jewish clergy and Pharisees look for a way to kill Jesus.

Unknown woman anoints Jesus on his head. – **A preview of Jesus as Messiah or "Anointed One"**

Judas goes to Jewish clergy and offers to betray Jesus.

Disciples prepare for Passover meal.

At beginning of Passover meal, Jesus announces and denounces Judas' betrayal.

Giving out bread, Jesus says, "Take; this is my body."

Giving out wine, Jesus says, "This is my blood of the covenant, which is poured out for many."

Gathered on Mount of Olives, Jesus tells disciples they will all desert his cause after his death.

Peter protests his loyalty; Jesus foretells his three denials; Peter asserts he will not deny.

Jesus prays while disciples sleep and Jesus upbraids Peter. – **Why does the Roman Church keep picking on Peter?**

Judas arrives with police, betrays Jesus with a kiss, and Jesus is arrested. – **Again, the identification with the arrest of the People of the Way in Rome by Roman police**

A certain young follower runs away naked. –

(Then all the disciples deserted him and ran away.) "And a young man was following him, wearing a shroud over his nude body, and they grabbed him. But he dropped the shroud and ran away naked."

This is a vignette about John Mark, possibly, and if so is a cameo appearance by the man to whom the gospel is dedicated. This verse does not appear in either Matthew or Luke.

Jesus' trial before the high priest and the Sanhedrin

When asked if he is the "Messiah, the Son of the Blessed One," Jesus says, "I am." – **When Jesus is arrested, he confesses his divine nature, and it is no longer hidden. The encouragement is to the Roman Christians to confess and not deny their faith in Jesus when arrested. They are to be faithful, even as Jesus was faithful, even unto death.**

Quote from Daniel 7:13

Jesus is condemned to death.

Peter denies Jesus three times. – **What purpose does this serve for the Roman Church?**

Chapter 15

Jesus is handed over to the Romans. – **The Passion of Jesus is the most faithfully copied section of this gospel by the writers of Matthew and Luke. There are very few changes made.**

Jesus' trial before Pilate

Jewish clergy incite crowd to ask that Barabbas be released and Jesus be crucified.

Roman soldiers torture Jesus.

Jesus is crucified.

Jesus is mocked by bystanders, Jewish clergy and Pharisees.

Jesus screams the first part of Psalm 22 and dies.

Curtain in Temple is torn in two.

Centurion says, "Truly this man was God's Son." – **Even a Roman centurion is forced to admit the divinity of Jesus.**

Women disciples are noted as being present.

Joseph of Arimathea buries Jesus in a tomb.

Chapter 16

Mary of Magdala, Mary of Nazareth and Salome go to tomb on Sunday to anoint Jesus' body. – **Whereas the story of the suffering and death of Jesus is copied meticulously by Matthew and Luke, the story of the resurrection varies in important details in the three gospels. One would think that the story of any event of this importance, the basis of the Christian faith, would also be uniform. Perhaps they understood physical death very well, but were still somewhat puzzled by physical resurrection.**

Tomb is open and one young man is sitting inside.

Young man tells women that Jesus is risen.

Young man tells women to tell disciples "and Peter" that Jesus will meet them in Galilee.

Women leave and say nothing to anyone because they are afraid. –

"And once they got outside, they ran away from the tomb, because great fear and excitement got the better of them. And they didn't breathe a word of it to anyone. Talk about terrified..."

This is the fourth and last passage in this gospel that is not copied by either Matthew or Luke. The point is that the secret must be kept until Jesus, the Son of God, the newly anointed Emperor of the Empire of God, makes his Triumphal Entry into Rome. Then they can tell everyone the Good News. And that is what they did when they wrote this gospel. There are no resurrection appearances by Jesus in the oldest Greek texts of Mark.

No appearances are needed because they firmly believed that Jesus was a god and his resurrection was a sure thing.

Conclusion

Several of the motifs in Mark described in this chapter have been bounced around in academic circles for decades. The secret messiahship of Jesus is old news. The location of the writing of this gospel in Rome is fairly common. Mark has been called the "gospel of many miracles" for a long time. The longer ending of the gospel has been declared unoriginal for over a hundred years.

What is relatively new in this chapter is the emphasis on: the "Empire of God" as the earthly arena to be shared with the Emperor Jesus tomorrow; speculation that Mark may have been written first in Latin, then translated into Greek; the theological influence of Paul; the identification of the Roman church with John the Baptist in his arrest and martyrdom and with the seed lying underground, waiting for the moment to push through to the light of God.

Chapter 4
Matthew Is the Jewish-Egyptian Gospel of Alexandria

The Gospel of Matthew is the gospel of the Jewish Brothers and Sisters in Alexandria, Egypt. This is what the early church members in Alexandria called themselves. It is their corporate expression of faith, written around 73-75 CE by a very literate scribe and dedicated to Matthew (a.k.a. Levi), the disciple. Some of the stories about Jesus may conceivably have come from Matthew – one tradition says his ministry was in Africa – but the odds are great that Matthew himself was illiterate, even though he was reputed to be a toll collector in and from Capernaum.

The Gospel dedicated to Matthew is a "manual of Christian discipline" in which Jesus is portrayed as the new-and-improved Moses, leader of the new-and-improved Judaism. He is described particularly as the fulfillment of God's will disclosed in the Hebrew Bible. Jesus is presented as Israel's royal Messiah and Savior, but totally human, who teaches his followers, the true Israel, the secrets they need to know to gain divine forgiveness and fellowship in the Kingdom of Heaven.

The number five (5) is very important in this gospel. There are five main divisions of the book. There are five discourses of Jesus, a note-worthy feature of this gospel, and they are collections of teachings on specific themes. The Sermon on the Mount is the first, and it's about right living. In the tenth (10th) chapter are instructions for missionary disciples. Chapter Thirteen (13) contains a slew of new parables of the Kingdom of Heaven. The subject of sincere discipleship is explored in Chapter Eighteen (18), and the end of the present age is the theme of Chapters Twenty-four (24) and Twenty-five (25). The writers seem to have deliberately built their gospel around these five great discourses as though their object was especially to show the fullness of Jesus' teaching. It is significant that the *Torah* or Pentateuch was for centuries called the "Five Books of Moses."

The Gospel dedicated to Matthew may tell us more about the Brothers and Sisters of Alexandria, their needs and hopes, than it tells us about the historical Jesus. They needed Jesus to be the greatest teacher, who dispensed crucial knowledge for life and life after death. They did not need Jesus to save them from the Romans as the Roman Church did. They were well-educated and well-heeled and didn't need Jesus to tell them what to do with their money, as the Antiochian Church did.

The Gospel dedicated to Mark sailed over from Rome and constitutes 60% of this gospel. The original material in this Jewish-Egyptian Gospel comes mostly from the Hebrew Bible and Egyptian mythology, as well as stories from eyewitnesses, possibly even Matthew. Therefore, this gospel becomes the third layer of the Synoptic Gospel cake, resting on top of the Roman Gospel, which rests on top of Paul's theology. There are no known copies of this gospel that were made before the middle of the fourth century. The scribe for the Brothers and Sisters of Alexandria was probably a well-educated Jewish man of means, well-versed in Greek. The gospel was written in eleventh-grade Greek. It has twenty-eight (28) chapters and is considerably longer than Mark.

Two very important themes run through this Jewish-Egyptian Gospel, both of which contrast with the Roman Gospel. First, Jesus is a human being of the lineage of David, and he could do miracles like Moses did. Jesus is presented as the greatest teacher of all time. This is a major Jewish correction to the Roman Gospel. Secondly, the "Kingdom of Heaven" is a future kingdom in the afterlife, not on this planet, which begins when one dies or when the Earth is destroyed, whichever comes first. This is a major Egyptian correction to the first gospel, reflecting the philosophy and theology behind the pyramids of the pharaohs. The ancient Egyptian concern with the afterlife, seen in the pyramids, is an important theme in this gospel.

The Gospel of Alexandria reflects its environment. In the physical sense, Alexandria was situated on the Mediterranean coast of Egypt on a thin strip of land with a large lake or lagoon on the south side. Its generous port was the second busiest in the Roman Empire. The port featured the famous Lighthouse of Alexandria, one of the seven wonders of the ancient world. There were many beautiful buildings in the city, and there was the great library, the repository of tens of thousands of ancient documents. Architecture and culture were heavily influenced by the Greeks who built Alexandria.

Historically speaking, Alexander the Great was the Greek emperor who conquered Egypt in 332 BCE and founded Alexandria the same year. Nine years later, Alexander died and his vast empire was divided among his Greek generals. Ptolemy was given Egypt and proclaimed himself king of Egypt. He established his capital in Alexandria. During his reign and those of his dynasty, Alexandria became one of the greatest cultural centers of ancient times. The last of his dynasty was Queen Cleopatra VII, who married Mark Anthony, the co-emperor of the Roman Empire in 37 BCE. Cleopatra and Anthony joined forces against Octavian (later Augustus Caesar) but were defeated in the sea Battle of Actium in 31 BCE, after which they both committed suicide. In 30 BCE, Egypt became a province of the Roman Empire. Vespasian (69-79 CE) was the emperor when the Gospel dedicated to Matthew was written.

In terms of demographics, ethnic Greeks probably were still providing local leadership in Alexandria, even though they were a small minority of the populace. Ethnic Egyptians made up the majority in the city of nine hundred thousand (900,000) residents. However, there was a large minority of ethic Jews present, living in the Delta section of the city. The families of some of these Jews had lived in Alexandria since soon after the city was founded. Other Jews migrated to the city to avoid the constant conflict which took place in Judea. Even more Jews fled to Alexandria after the Romans destroyed Jerusalem in 70 CE. Almost all the Brothers and Sisters of Alexandria were ethnic Jews, and it was a strong patriarchal society. Their ancestors had built several synagogues in the Delta section with their own hands and their own money. The Brothers and Sisters began meeting in one of these synagogues on Sunday until they were prohibited from meeting there by the Rabbi and the local council of Pharisees. This created a great deal of animosity, which they reflected in their gospel.

The first-century Alexandrians were steeped in Greek philosophy. Persian Zoroastrianism was known and Greek Gnostic thought forms were very evident, but they competed with Jewish thought forms and Egyptian culture and heritage. Learning was the most valuable currency. This is evidenced by the presence of the magnificent library. There was a relatively much higher literacy rate among the Alexandrians than in other cities of the Empire, and they all spoke Greek.

There were hundreds of gods recognized and worshiped in Alexandria, especially Isis and Osiris. The Brothers and Sisters in Alexandria were unique in their fierce monotheism and worship of Yahweh only. At the time they wrote their gospel, they were not interested in starting a new religion based on Jesus, but they were interested in propagating a new and improved version of Judaism. Emperor worship was not practiced with much enthusiasm in Alexandria. Many religions were legal in the Empire, including Judaism, but Christianity (as it was later called) was considered an illegitimate sect of Judaism and therefore illegal.

The Jewish population of Alexandria was defiantly monotheistic, recognizing the existence of only one God, and that was Yahweh. The Jews had a Greek translation of *Torah* and *Neviim* (the "Law and the Prophets"), called the Septuagint, since Ptolemy II had it translated by seventy rabbis in 250 BCE.

They were also well aware of the mythological literature of this era. The story of Dionysus was a part of Egyptian-Greek mythology and was well-known around the Mediterranean in the first century. Its influence is seen throughout Matthew in the events of Jesus' life. In brief form, Dionysus was the son of Zeus, the king of the gods on Mt. Olympus, and Semele, the virgin princess of Thebes, Egypt. When Hera, Zeus' wife, learned of his dalliance with a human, she sent the Titans to kill the baby, but they were unsuccessful. When Dionysus was grown, he performed many miracles and invented wine-making and taught others how to make wine. Eventually, the Titans caught up with him and tortured him and killed him, but Zeus resurrected him and brought him to Mt. Olympus and gave him the seat at his right hand.

Conclusion

Some scholars have theorized that the Gospel dedicated to Matthew was written in Antioch of Syria. Others have speculated that its origin was elsewhere. The theory of this book is that this gospel was the product of the Church of Alexandria, and here are a few of the arguments:

1. **This is a** Jewish gospel written in a Jewish community. Alexandria had more Jewish inhabitants in the first century than Judea

and the Galilee combined and more than any other city in the Roman Empire.

2. **Matthew is the** only one of the three Synoptic Gospels that insists on Jewish monotheism and does not affirm the divinity of Jesus.

3. **The Egyptian influence** is seen in changing the "Empire of God" in Mark to the "Kingdom of Heaven" in Matthew.

4. **Two Jewish-Egyptian heroes,** Joseph and Moses, are lionized in this gospel, Joseph becoming the name of the "father" of Jesus, and Moses becoming the prototype of Jesus.

5. **In the birth** story of Jesus in Matthew, Joseph takes Jesus and Mary to Egypt for safety. Antioch and other Christian communities would have had little interest in recording such a trip.

Chapter 5
Original Content of the Gospel Dedicated to Matthew

When the Roman Gospel dedicated to Mark arrived in Alexandria and got into the hands of the literate Alexandrian Church, it must have been a momentous occasion and a cause for much rejoicing. They had to be impressed that the Roman Church had taken a great risk to write the first account of Jesus' ministry from his baptism to his resurrection. In fact, they were so impressed that they included almost all of the Roman Gospel in their gospel. A full sixty percent (60%) of their gospel is taken from Mark; some of it verbatim, some of it edited, some of it moved in the narrative sequence.

One can imagine that the Alexandrians were amused at the low quality of Greek in which Mark was written in Rome. They could have decided rather quickly that they could write a better gospel than Mark, with better Greek and different emphases. They would have been appalled that the Roman Church deified Jesus. They would have thought it rather juvenile of the Roman Church that they believed that Jesus was going to come marching into Rome tomorrow as the new emperor of the Empire of God.

They would have felt it to be their duty to add some important sections to the Roman Gospel. They added a birth story and resurrection appearances. They added sermons and teachings by Jesus. They added secret parables in keeping with the influence of Gnosticism in their Greek culture. They added comparisons between Jesus and Moses. All these things and more make up the other forty percent (40%) of the Gospel dedicated to Matthew, their new content.

The following is the material that is original in the Alexandrian Gospel. Some of this material in Matthew was used by the scribe of the Gospel dedicated to Luke. That material is presented in Chapter 7 in the presentation of the impact of Matthew on the Antiochian Gospel.

Jewish Version Of Jesus' Family Tree
(Matthew 1:1-17)

> This is the family tree of Jesus the Messiah, who was a descendant of David and Abraham.
>
> Abraham was the father of Isaac, Isaac of Jacob, Jacob of Judah and his brothers, and Judah and Tamar were the parents of Perez and Zerah. Perez was the father of Hezron, Hezron of Ram, and Ram of Amminadab, Amminadab of Nahshon, Nahshon of Salmon, and Salmon and Rahab were the parents of Boaz. Boaz and Ruth were the parents of Obed, and Obed was the father of Jesse, and Jesse of King David.
>
> David and Uriah's wife were the parents of Solomon. Solomon was the father of Rehoboam, Rehoboam of Abijah, Abijah of Asaph, Asaph of Jehoshaphat, Jehoshaphat of Joram, Joram of Uzziah, Uzziah of Jotham, Jotham of Ahaz, Ahaz of Hezekiah, Hezekiah of Manasseh, Manasseh of Amos, Amos of Josiah, and Josiah was the father of Jechoniah and his brothers, at the time of the exile to Babylon.
>
> After the Babylonian exile, Jechoniah was the father of Salathiel, Salathiel of Zerubbabel, Zerubbabel of Abiud, Abiud of Eliakim, Eliakim of Azor, Azor of Zadok, Zadok of Achim, Achim of Eliud, Eliud of Eleazar, Eleazar of Matthan, Matthan of Jacob. And Jacob was the father of Joseph, the husband of Mary, who was the mother of Jesus, who is known as the Messiah.
>
> In sum, the generations from Abraham to David come to fourteen, those from David to the Babylonian exile equal fourteen, and those from the Babylonian exile to the Messiah amount to fourteen also.

There are several reasons for starting this gospel with a family tree. It is important to place Jesus in the royal line of David. Beginning the tree with Abraham indicates this gospel comes from a Jewish community. With the ninth word of this gospel, Jesus is established as "the Messiah," but this does not indicate divinity. In the Jewish mind, messiahs are "raised up" by Yahweh (rather then "sent down from heaven") from among the people and anointed for special purposes. Even Cyrus the Great, the Persian ruler who sent the Jews home from Babylon, is called "Messiah" in Isaiah

45:1. Notice that the tree goes to Joseph, not Mary, and this is the first mention of Joseph in the gospels, since he is not mentioned in Mark. It is possible that Joseph is the name given to the "father" of Jesus by the Church of Alexandria as a parallel and tribute to the Joseph of Genesis, the Jewish-Egyptian hero. Also, fourteen (as in fourteen generations) is a number divisable by seven, and seven is a holy and complete number.

A Message From God To Joseph
(Matthew 1:18-25)

> While Jesus' mother Mary was engaged to Joseph, but before they slept together, she was found to be pregnant by the sacred breath of life. Her husband Joseph was a just man and unwilling to expose her publicly, so he was planning to break off their engagement quietly.
>
> While he was thinking about this, a messenger of the Lord surprised him in a dream, saying, "Joseph, of the house of David, don't hesitate to take Mary as your wife, since the sacred breath of life is responsible for her pregnancy. She will give birth to a son, and you shall name him Jesus, which means 'he will save his people from their sins.'"
>
> All of this has happened so the prediction of the Lord given by the prophet would come true:
>
>> Look, the virgin shall conceive a child
>> and she will give birth to a son,
>> and they shall name him Emmanuel,
>> (which means, "God is with us.")
>
> Joseph woke up and did what the messenger of the Lord told him. He took (Mary) as his wife. He did not sleep with her until she had given birth to a son.

The connection between Joseph of Bethlehem and the Jewish-Egyptian Joseph in Genesis begins here. Just as the son of Jacob was a dreamer and one who interpreted dreams, this Joseph is also one who has dreams and interprets them for himself. In Hebrew "Yosef" and Aramaic "Yoses" means "he who adds" or "Good-with-Figures." Here we have also the first of many references to the prophets of the Hebrew Bible. In fact, compared to the Roman Gospel, the Alexandrian Gospel contains twenty-one (21) additional quotes from the Septuagint, the Greek translation of the Hebrew Bible, indicating the Jewish nature of the Church of Alexandria.

Visit Of Astrologers From Persian Area
(Matthew 2:1-12)

Jesus was born in Bethlehem, in Judea, when Herod was king. Astrologers from the East came to Jerusalem, saying, "Where is the newborn king of the Judeans? For we have seen his star in the East, and have come to pay him homage." When King Herod heard this, he was visibly shaken, and all Jerusalem along with him. He assembled all the ranking priests and local experts. He pressed them for information: "Where is the Messiah supposed to be born?" They told him, "In Bethlehem of Judea." This is how it is put by the prophet:

And you, Bethlehem, in the province of Judah,
you are by no means least among the rulers of Judah;
for out of you shall come a ruler
who will shepherd my people Israel.

Then Herod called the astrologers together secretly and learned from them the precise date the star became visible. Then he sent them to Bethlehem, with these instructions: "Go make a careful search for the child, and when you have found out where he is, report to me, so I can come and pay him homage."

They listened to what the king had to say and they continued on their way. And there guiding them on was the star that they had seen in the East. It led them forward until it came to a standstill above where the child lay. When they saw the star, they were beside themselves with joy. They arrived at the dwelling and they saw the child with Mary his mother. They fell down and paid him homage. Then they opened their treasure chests and presented him gifts, gold and incense and myrrh. And because they had been alerted in a dream not to return to Herod, they journeyed back to their own country by a different route.

These are Zoroastrian mobeds (priests) from the Parthian Empire. They are probably "wise" but are not "kings." Obviously, Zoroastrian religion and its components are known in Alexandria. In the middle of the passage is another new quote from a prophet.

The Family Escapes To Egypt
(Matthew 2:13-18)

A messenger of the Lord appeared to Joseph in a dream and said, "Get ready, take the child and his mother, and flee to Egypt, and stay there till I give you further instructions. For Herod is determined to hunt the child down and destroy him." He got ready and took the child and his mother under cover of night and departed for Egypt.

They remained there until the death of Herod. This happened so the Lord's prediction spoken by the prophet would come true: "Out of Egypt I have called my son."

When Herod realized he had been duped by the astrologers, he was outraged, and he issued a death warrant for all the male children in Bethlehem and surrounding region who were two years old or under, according to the date that he had learned from the astrologers. Then the prediction by the prophet Jeremiah came true:

> A voice was heard in Ramah,
> mourning and bitter grieving:
> Rachel weeping for her children.
> She refused to be consoled,
> because they were no more.

Joseph has another dream and then is responsible for getting Jesus, "the new Israel," to Egypt, just as Joseph in Genesis is responsible for getting the old Israel, Jacob and all his family, to Egypt. In the Greek-Egyptian story of Dionysus, when Hera found out that her husband, Zeus, had a baby son with the virgin princess of Thebes, she sent her minions to kill the baby. They were unsuccessful at that time. The story of "the Slaughter of the Innocents" in Bethlehem has no historical verification. This passage has two new quotes from Hebrew prophets.

Joseph And Mary And Jesus Settle Down In Nazareth
(Matthew 2:19-23)

> But when Herod died, a messenger of the Lord appeared in a dream to Joseph in Egypt, saying, "Get ready, take the child and his mother, and return to the land of Israel, for those who sought the child's life are dead." He got ready and took the child and his mother, and returned to the land of Israel. But when he heard that (Herod) Archelaus reigned over Judea in place of his father Herod ("the Great"), he was afraid to go there. He was instructed in a dream to go to Galilee. So he went there and settled in the town called Nazareth. So the prediction spoken by the prophets came true, "He shall be called a Nazorean."

Yet another Joseph dream and interpretation. Then Jesus, the new and improved Moses, comes out of Egypt in a Second Exodus and this time makes it into the Promised Land. Notice that there is no hint that Joseph and Mary lived in Nazareth before the birth of Jesus. Indeed, since Joseph is a member of the tribe of Judah, it is implied that they were living near Bethlehem at the time of Jesus' birth. Nazareth becomes their new home because Joseph feels that Herod's son in Jerusalem is a threat.

John's Baptism At The Jordan River
(Matthew 3:7-10)

> But when he saw that many of the Pharisees and Sadducees were coming for baptism, he said, "You wriggling mass of baby poisonous snakes! Who warned you to flee from the impending doom? Well then, start producing fruit suitable for a change of heart, and don't even think of saying to yourselves, 'We have Abraham as our father.' Let me tell you, God can raise up children for Abraham right out of these rocks. Even now the axe is aimed at the root of the trees. Every tree therefore that does not produce good fruit is cut down and thrown into the fire."

This is Alexandria's opening volley against the Pharisees (and Sadducees) who had shut them out of their synagogues on Sundays. The Roman Gospel has the story of the baptism, but this attack on the Pharisees at the baptism is new in this Jewish Gospel.

Jesus' Temptation And Profession Of Faith
(Matthew 4:1-11)

> Then Jesus was guided by the breath of life into the Wilderness, to be tempted by the Devil. He ate nothing for forty days and forty nights. He was very hungry.
>
> The Tempter came and said, "If you are God's son, order these stones to turn into bread."
>
> Jesus answered him, "It is written, 'One is not to live on bread alone, but on every word that comes from the mouth of God.'"
>
> Then the Devil took him to the Holy City, and set him on the highest point (of the wall around) the Temple area, and said to him, "If you are God's son, jump off; remember, it is written, 'He will give orders about you to his messengers,' and 'With their hands they will catch you, so that you will not even stub your toe on a stone.'"
>
> Jesus said, "Again it is written, 'Do not put the Lord your God to the test.'"
>
> Again, the Devil took him to a very high mountain, and showed him all the kingdoms of the world and their splendor, and said to him, "I will give you authority over all this if you will kneel down and pay homage to me."

Finally Jesus said to him, "Get out of here, Satan! Remember, it is written, 'You are to pay homage to the Lord your God, and you are to serve him alone.'"

Then the Devil let him alone. Then messengers from the heavens arrived out of nowhere and looked after Jesus.

Here is a significant expansion of the temptation story. In Mark, just the event itself is noted. Here, the Jewish nature of the authors is reflected in an important way. All of Jesus' answers to the temptations are from the great "Shema" which begins in Deuteronomy 6. This is the first scripture passage taught to and learned by Jewish children. The "tempter" is also called "the devil" and "Satan," indicating reliance again on Zoroastrianism. Notice that two of the temptations begin with "if you are God's son," and that Jesus doesn't bite either time at the name or the temptation.

Jesus' Return To Galilee
(Matthew 4:12-17)

When Jesus heard that John had been locked up, he headed for Galilee, filled with the power of the sacred breath of life. He had left Nazareth to go and make his home in Capernaum by the Sea (of Galilee), in the territory of Zebulun and Naphtali, so that the word spoken by the prophet Isaiah (9:1-2) would come true:

Land of Zebulun, land of Naphtali,
On the road by the sea, across the Jordan,
Galilee of the pagans!
The people who sat in darkness
have seen a great light,
Those who have wasted away in the shadow of death,
For them a light has risen.

This passage contains another new quote from Hebrew prophetic literature.

Blessings: Like The Ancient Covenant Renewal Festival
(Matthew 5:1-12)

Facing the crowd (up on the steep hillside), he sat down and began to speak, and this is what he spoke to them:

Blessed are the poor in the breath of life, for the
Kingdom of Heaven belongs to them.
Blessed are those who mourn, for they will be comforted.

Blessed are the gentle, for they will inherit the earth.
Blessed are those who hunger and thirst for justice,
for they will have a feast.
Blessed are the merciful, for they will receive mercy.
Blessed are those with undefiled hearts, for they will see God.
Blessed are the peacemakers,
for they will be known as children of God.
Blessed are those who have suffered persecution
for the sake of justice,
for the Kingdom of Heaven belongs to them.
Blessed are you when people revile you
and persecute you and spread malicious gossip
about you because of me.
Rejoice and be glad! Your compensation is great in the heavens.
Remember that this is how they persecuted
the prophets who preceded you.

The "Sermon on the Mount" begins with Jesus on the mountainside, speaking "the word of the Lord" to the people, just as Moses on the mountain gave the Israelites the "Law." Jesus gives the blessings in good Hebrew tradition. Moses' "ten commandments" may have been in the form of blessings and curses originally. The Israelites once gathered annually in Shechem for the Covenant Renewal Festival where blessings and curses were shouted from the sides of Mt. Ebal and Mt. Gerizim. It is notable that this well-to-do community does not need Jesus to direct blessing to the poor, but to the "poor in spirit." Here also is the first mention of the "Kingdom of Heaven," in great contrast to the "Empire of God" in the Roman Gospel. For this Jewish-Egyptian church, the Kingdom of Heaven is up there, out there among the stars, the place of life after death.

About Discipleship
(Matthew 5:13-16)

"You are the salt of the earth. Salt is good, but if salt has lost its zing, how shall it be made salty again? It has no further use except to be thrown out and stomped on.

"You are the light of the world. A city sitting on top of a mountain cannot be hidden. Nor do people light a lamp and put it under a bushel basket but on a lampstand, where it sheds light for all in the house. That is how your light is to shine in the presence of others, so they can see your good deeds and give glory to your Father in the heavens.

The Hebrew model puts Yahweh on all three floors of house: the basement is Sheol, the place of the dead; the first floor is the ground floor on the flat Earth, where life goes on; the second floor is the sky or the heavens, which you can almost touch from the tops of mountains. The Egyptian model puts Yahweh in the heavens exclusively by using the phrase "your Father in the heavens," which is repeated several times in the following sections.

Promoting A Deeper Spirituality
(Matthew 5:17-20)

> "Do not imagine that I have come to cancel the Teaching (*Torah*) or the Prophets (*Neviim*). I haven't come to cancel (them) but to fulfill (them). I swear to you, before the world disappears, not one little letter, not one dot or any decorative piece of any letter, will disappear from the Teaching until it's all over. Whoever ignores one of the most trivial of these teachings and teaches others to do so, shall be called trivial in the Kingdom of Heaven. But whoever acts on them and teaches them shall be called great in the Kingdom of Heaven. Let me tell you, unless your spirituality goes beyond that of the scholars and Pharisees, you will never set foot in the Kingdom of Heaven.

Respect for the Hebrew Bible (in the form of the Greek Septuagint since the Alexandrians spoke Greek) was very important to this church as it tried to show that their faith was in a new and improved Judaism. They also need Jesus to issue a condemnation of the Church's enemies in Alexandria, the rabbis and Pharisees who have prevented them from gathering in "their" synagogues on Sunday mornings.

Deeper Spirituality And Appropriate Expression Of Anger
(Matthew 5:21-26)

> "You know that our ancestors were told, 'You shall not murder' and 'Whoever murders will be subject to judgment.' But I tell you that those who are angry with a brother or sister (read "fellow church member") will be liable to judgment. Those who insult a brother or sister will be brought before a tribunal. And whoever says, 'You idiot!' deserves the fires of the Valley of Hinnom. So, even if you happen to be offering your gift at the altar, and there remember that your brother or sister has some claim against you, leave your gift there before the altar. First go and be reconciled to your brother or sister, and then come back and offer your gift.

"When you are about to appear with your accuser before the magistrate, do your best to settle with him on the way, or else your accuser might drag you up before the judge, and the judge turn you over to the jailer, and the jailer throw you in prison. I tell you, you will never get out of there till you have paid the last red cent.

This is the first of five (5) passages where Jesus is presented explicitly as the new and improved Moses. In each passage Jesus tells what the "old Moses" said, and then gives his "new Moses" version. The scene has already been set with the mountain setting and the blessings (5:1-12). The entire "Sermon on the Mount" is divided into five parts to mirror the "five books of Moses" which are the *Torah*. In the following four passages, only the "old" and the "new" are shown here.

Deeper Spirituality And Adultery
(Matthew 5:27-30)

"You know that our ancestors were told, 'You shall not commit adultery.' But I say to you that those who leer at a woman and desire her have already committed adultery with her in their hearts...

New and improved Moses II

Deeper Spirituality And Giving Your Word Of Honor
(Matthew 5:33-37)

"Again, you know that our ancestors were told, 'You shall not break a covenant', and 'Covenants made invoking the name of the Lord shall be kept.' But I say to you: do not swear at all...

New and improved Moses III

Deeper Spirituality And Reverse Payback
(Matthew 5:38-42)

"You know that our ancestors were told, 'An eye for an eye' and 'A tooth for a tooth.' But I say to you: Do not react violently against the one who is evil...

New and improved Moses IV

Deeper Spirituality And Love Of Enemies
(Matthew 5:43-48)

"You know we once were told, 'You shall love your neighbor' and 'You shall hate your enemy.' But I say to you: Love your enemies. Pray for those who persecute you…"

New and improved Moses V

Deeper Spirituality And Charitable Giving
(Matthew 6:1-4)

"Take care that you don't flaunt your religion in public to be noticed by others. Otherwise, you will have no recognition from your Father in the heavens. For example, when you give to charity, don't bother to toot your own horn as some phony pietists do in houses of worship and on the streets. They are seeking human recognition. I swear to you, their grandstanding is its own reward. Instead, when you give to charity, do not let your left hand know what your right hand is doing, so your acts of charity may remain hidden. And your Father, who has an eye for the hidden, will applaud you.

Clearly, the Brothers and Sisters have Jesus referring to contemporary practices of Pharisees in Alexandria.

Deeper Spirituality And Prayer
(Matthew 6:5-15)

"When you pray, you must not act like the phonies. They love to stand up and pray in houses of worship and on street corners, so they can show off in public. I swear to you, their prayers have been answered! When you pray, go into a room by yourself and shut the door behind you. Then pray to your Father, the hidden one. And your Father, with his eye for the hidden, will applaud you. And when you pray, you should not babble on as the pagans do. They imagine that the length of their prayers will command attention. So, do not imitate them. After all, your Father knows what you need before you ask."

And Jesus said, "When you pray, say:
Our Father in the heavens,
your name be revered.
Impose your Kingdom,
enact your will on earth,
as you have in the heavens.

Provide us with the bread
we need day by day.
Forgive our debts
to the extent we have forgiven
everyone in debt to us.
And please don't subject us to test after test,
but rescue us from evil.

"For if you forgive others their failures and offenses, your Father in the heavens also will forgive yours. But if you do not forgive others their failures and mistakes, neither will your Father forgive yours.

"Phonies" is the favorite name for Pharisees in the Alexandrian church.

Deeper Spirituality And Fasting
(Matthew 6:16-18)

"When you fast, do not make a spectacle of your remorse as the phonies do. As you know, they make their faces unrecognizable so they may be publicly recognized. I swear to you, they have gotten what they wanted. But when you fast, comb your hair and wash your face, so your fasting may go unrecognized in public. But it will be recognized by your Father, the hidden one, and your Father, who has an eye for the hidden, will applaud you.

More reference is made to contemporary practices of Pharisees in Alexandria.

Deeper Spirituality And Living Life In The Present
(Matthew 6:19-34)

Deeper Spirituality And Fairness
(Matthew 7:1-5)

On Profaning The Holy
(Matthew 7:6)

Answer To Prayer
(Matthew 7:7-11)

Golden Rule
(Matthew 7:12)

> "Treat people the way you want them to treat you, for that is the theme of all the Teaching and the Prophets."

The Alexandrian church summarizes the Hebrew Bible in one sentence.

Narrow Gate
(Matthew 7:13-14)

> "Try to get in through the narrow gate. Wide and smooth is the road that leads to destruction. The majority are taking that route. Narrow and rough is the way that leads to life. Only a minority discover it."

A reversal of thinking about the Zoroastrian bridge called "Chinvat." The Persian bridge from life to death was wide for the righteous but narrow as a razor blade for the unrighteous. The Jewish-Christians in Alexandria see it just the opposite and as a minority are traveling the narrow way to life.

On Discernment
(Matthew 7:15-20)

> "Be on the lookout for phony prophets, who make their pitch disguised as sheep. Inside they are really voracious wolves. You will know who they are by what they produce. Since when do people pick grapes from thorn bushes, or figs from thistles?
>
> "Every healthy tree produces choice fruit, but the diseased tree produces rotten fruit. A healthy tree cannot produce rotten fruit, nor can a diseased tree produce choice fruit. Every tree that does not produce choice fruit is cut down and thrown into the fire. Remember, you will know who they are by what they produce."

Probably referring negatively to rabbis within the Shammai Pharisee tradition in Alexandria.

On Salvation
(Matthew 7:21-23)

Conclusion On Importance Of Building One's Faith Carefully
(Matthew 7:24-27)

Jesus Cures A Roman Officer's Slave
(Matthew 8:5-13)

> When he finished preaching to the people, he went back to Capernaum. A Roman officer (in town) came to Jesus, pleading with him urgently, saying, "Master, my servant is lying at my house paralyzed, in terrible pain."
>
> Jesus said, "I will go and cure him." The Roman officer answered, "Sir, I don't deserve to have you in my house. Just say the word, and let my slave be cured. After all, I myself am under orders, with soldiers under me. I order one to go and he goes. I order another to come and he comes. And (I order) my slave to do something and he does it."
>
> When Jesus heard this he was amazed at him, and turned and said to the crowd that followed him, "Let me tell you, I have not found such faith in a single Israelite! I predict that many will come from east and west, and from north and south, and dine with Abraham, Isaac, and Jacob in the Kingdom of Heaven, while those who think the Kingdom belongs to them will be thrown where it is utterly dark. There will be weeping and grinding of teeth out there."
>
> Jesus said to the Roman officer, "Be on your way. Your trust will be the measure of the results." The servant was cured at that precise moment.

In praise of a Roman, in disdain of the Pharisees. At this early stage, the Church of Alexandria was having no problem with Roman persecution of Christians.

Wanna-be Followers Of Jesus
(Matthew 8:19-22)

Curing Two Blind Men And A Man With Multiple Problems
(Matthew 9:27-35)

Encouragement To Disciples
(Matthew 10:26-40)

"Don't be afraid of the opposition. After all, there is nothing veiled that won't be unveiled, or hidden that won't be make known (when it) comes to light. What I say to you in darkness, say in the light. What you have said in darkness will be heard in the light. What you hear whispered in your ear and what you have whispered behind closed doors, announce from the rooftops.

"I tell you, don't fear those who kill the body, (because they) cannot kill the soul. Fear the one who can kill both body and soul and then has authority to cast into the Valley of Hinnom. Can't you buy two sparrows for a penny? Yet not one of them will fall to the earth without the consent of your Father. In fact, even the hairs of your head have all been counted. Don't be timid. You're worth more than a flock of sparrows.

"I tell you, everyone who acknowledges me in public, I will acknowledge in front of my Father in the heavens. But whoever disowns me in public, I also will disown in the presence of my Father in the heavens.

"Don't get the idea that I came to bring peace to the earth. I haven't come to bring peace but a sword. In fact I have come

to pit a man against his father,
a daughter against her mother,
a daughter-in-law against her mother-in-law.
One person's foes will be members
of that person's own household.

"If you love your father or mother more than me, you aren't worthy of me. If you love your son or daughter more than me, you aren't worthy of me. Unless you take up your cross and follow me, you aren't worthy of me. By finding your life, you'll lose it, and by losing your life for my sake, you'll find it.

"Whoever accepts you accepts me, and whoever accepts me accepts the one who sent me. Whoever accepts a prophet as a prophet will be treated like a prophet. Whoever accepts a virtuous person as a virtuous person will be treated like a virtuous person. Whoever gives so much as a cup of cool water to one of these little ones, because the little one is a follower of mine, I swear to you, such a person won't go unrewarded."

Evidence that there was much family turmoil caused by this new Jewish-Christian community within the Jewish Delta section of Alexandria.

Jesus And John The Baptist
(Matthew 11:1-19)

(After the disciples left, Jesus) moved on from there to teach and proclaim in the towns (of Galilee).

When John heard in prison of all these things the Messiah was doing, he sent word by his disciples to ask, "Are you the one who is to come, or shall we to wait for another?"

Jesus answered them, "Go report to John what you have seen and heard:

the blind see again,
the lame walk,
lepers are cleansed
the deaf hear,
the dead are raised,
and the poor have the good news preached to them.
Blessed are those who don't take offense at me."

After John's disciples had gone, Jesus began to talk about John to the crowds: "What did you go out to the wilderness to gawk at? A reed shaking in the wind? What did you really go out to see? A man dressed in fancy clothes? But wait! Those who dress fashionably and live in luxury are found in palaces. Come on, what did you go out to see? A prophet? Yes, that's what you went out to see, yet someone more than a prophet. This is the one of whom it was written,

Here is my messenger,
Whom I send on ahead of you to prepare your way before you.
I tell you, among those born of women none is greater
than John the Baptist. Yet, the least in the
Kingdom of Heaven is greater than he.

Since John arrived, the Kingdom of Heaven has been breaking in violently, and violent people are attempting to break into it violently. You see, the Prophets and even the Teaching predicted everything that was to happen prior to John's time. And if you are willing to admit it, John is the Elijah who was expected. Anyone here with two ears had better listen!

What do the people of this generation remind me of? They are like children sitting in the marketplaces who call out to others:

We played the flute for you, but you would not dance.

We sang a dirge but you would not mourn.

Just remember, John the Baptist appeared on the scene, eating nothing and drinking nothing, and they say, 'He is demented.' The Son of Adam appeared on the scene both eating and drinking; and they say, 'There is a glutton and a drunk, a crony of toll collectors and sinners!' Indeed, wisdom is vindicated by all her children."

There is not the identification with John the Baptist by Alexandria like there was in Rome. In the Roman Gospel, John is arrested very early in the narrative. In Alexandria, John's story is much less important.

Condemnation Of Galilean Towns
(Matthew 11:20-24)

Jesus Prays
(Matthew 11:25-26)

At that point he said, "I praise you, Father, Lord of the heavens and the earth, because you have hidden these things from the wise and learned but revealed them to the untutored. Yes indeed, Father, because this is the way you want it."

An interesting reference to Gnosticism and secret knowledge.

Father And Son
(Matthew 11:27)

Comfort For The Weary
(Matthew 11:28-30)

Jesus Cautions The Pharisees
About Looking For Signs From The Heavens
(Matthew 12:38-42)

Teaching About The Return Of Unclean Spirits
(Matthew 12:43-45)

Reason For Parables
(Matthew 13:13-17)

"That is why I tell them parables, so that:
They may look with eyes wide open but never really see,
and may listen with ears attuned but never really understand,
otherwise they might turn around and find forgiveness!

Moreover, in them the prophecy of Isaiah (6:9-10) comes true, the one which says:

You listen closely, yet you will never understand,
and you look intently but will never perceive.
For the mind of this people has grown dull,
and their ears are hard of hearing,
and they have shut their eyes,
otherwise they might actually see with their eyes,
and hear with their ears,
and understand with their minds,
and turn around and I would cure them.

Fortunate are your eyes because they see, and your ears because they hear. I swear to you, many prophets and righteous ones have longed to see what you see and didn't see it, and to hear what you hear and didn't hear it."

Gnosticism is about secret knowledge. There are twelve (12) new parables added in this gospel, compared to the Roman Gospel. Most of these twelve are not simple parables, but can be interpreted in a wide variety of ways. This Greek-thinking community needs Jesus to impart secret knowledge in these parables because this knowledge contains the keys to the gates of the Kingdom of Heaven.

Parable Of Weeds Mixed In With Wheat
(Matthew 13:24-30)

He spun out another parable for them: "The Kingdom of Heaven is like someone who sowed good (wheat) seed in his field. And while everyone was sleeping, his enemy came and scattered weed seed around in his wheat, and stole away. So when the crop sprouted and produced heads, the weeds appeared also.

The owner's slaves came and asked him, 'Master, didn't you sow good seed in your field? Then why are there weeds everywhere?'

He said to them, 'Some enemy has done this.'

The slaves said to him, 'Do you want us then to go and pull weeds?'

> He replied, 'No, lest in pulling the weeds you root up the wheat at the same time. Let them grow up together until the harvest. At harvest time I will tell the harvesters to gather the weeds first and bind them in bundles to burn, but gather the wheat into my granary.' Anyone here with two good ears had better listen."

Is this about the mixture of beliefs in the Jewish Delta section of Alexandria, with Jews and those who believed in a new and improved Judaism? Notice the sentence at the end about the "two good ears." It refers to the secret nature of this knowledge.

Parable Of Yeast Hidden In A Large Amount Of Bread Dough
(Matthew 13:33)

> The Kingdom of Heaven is like leaven which a woman took and concealed in fifty pounds of flour until it was all leavened.

Nowhere in the Old or New Testaments is leaven or yeast mentioned in a positive way. It is always negative. What does this parable mean? It's a secret!

Understanding The Parable Of The Weeds
(Matthew 13:36-43)

> Then his disciples said to him, "Explain to us the parable of the weeds of the field."

> This was his response: "The one who sows the good seed is the Son of Adam. The field is the world, and the good seed are those to whom the Kingdom of Heaven belongs. The weeds represent children of evil (personified). The enemy who sows (the weeds) is the Tempter, and the harvest is the end of the present age, and the harvesters are messengers of the heavens. Just as the weeds are gathered and destroyed by fire, that's how it will be at the end of the present age. The Son of Adam will send his messengers, and they will gather out of his Kingdom all the snares and subverters of the Teaching, and throw them into the fiery furnace. People in that place will weep and grind their teeth. Then those who are vindicated will be radiant like the sun in the Kingdom of their Father. Anyone here with two ears had better listen.

Probably a later addition to the gospel, since explanations of parables defeat the whole purpose of secret knowledge. Somebody couldn't resist condemning the enemy of the church to the "fiery furnace."

Parable Of Buried Family Heirlooms
(Matthew 13:44)

> The Kingdom of Heaven is like treasure hidden in a field. Someone finds it and covers it up again, and then, out of sheer joy, goes and sells every last possession and buys that field.

What does it mean? It's a secret!

Parable Of A Perfect Pearl
(Matthew 13:45-46)

> Similarly, the Kingdom of Heaven is like some trader looking for eautiful pearls. When that merchant finds one priceless pearl, he sells everything he owns and buys it.

What does it mean? It's a secret!

Parable Of A Net That Catches All Kinds Of Fish
(Matthew 13:47-50)

> Once more, the Kingdom of Heaven is like a net which is cast into the sea and catches all kinds of fish. When the net is full, they haul it ashore. Then they sit down and collect the good fish into baskets, but the worthless fish they throw away. This is how the present age will end. God's messengers will go out and separate the evil from the righteous, and throw the evil into the fiery furnace. People in that place will weep and grind their teeth.

Here we have the first mention in this gospel of the end of the "present age." Then, a reference to the division of the evil and the righteous and the punishment of the evil in the "fiery furnace." All this is language from Zoroastrianism.

Parable Of A Toastmaster
(Matthew 13:51-52)

> Do you understand all these things?" "Of course," they replied.
>
> He said to them, "That's why every scholar who is schooled in the Kingdom of Heaven is like a toastmaster who produces from his cellar something mature and something young."

This is Gnostic language being used to stress the importance of "knowing" the secrets of the Kingdom of Heaven.

Jesus And Simon Peter
(Matthew 16:17-19)

> Peter replied, "You are the Messiah, the Son of the living God!"
>
> And in response Jesus said to him, "Blessed are you, Simon son of Jonah! Because flesh and blood did not reveal this to you, but my Father in the heavens. Let me tell you, you are Peter, 'the Rock,' and on this very rock I will build my congregation, and the gates of the Place of the Dead will not be able to overpower it. I will give you the keys to the Kingdom of Heaven, and whatever you bind on earth shall be considered bound in the heavens, and whatever you release on earth shall be considered released in the heavens."

Alexandria treats Simon Peter better than Rome does. It is curious that the Jewish Gospel holds Peter in higher esteem than the Roman Gospel. This passage does not exist in the Roman Gospel, and Peter is the first "bishop" of the Roman Church in Roman Church tradition.

Question About Paying Temple Tax
(Matthew 17:24-27)

> Shortly after they arrived (home) in Capernaum, those who collect the Temple tax came to Peter and said, "Your teacher pays the Temple tax, doesn't he?" He said, "That's right."
>
> When he got to their home, Jesus anticipated what was on Peter's mind: "What are you thinking, Simon? On whom do secular rulers levy taxes and tolls? Do they levy them on their own people or on aliens?"

Peter said, "On aliens."

Jesus responded to him, "Then their own people are exempt. However, we don't want to get in trouble with them, so go down to the lake, and cast your line in, and take the first fish that comes up. Open its mouth you will find a coin. Take that and pay the (tax) for both of us."

This passage may indicate some competition between Jerusalem and Alexandria for supremacy as the city with the largest Jewish population. By the time this gospel is written, the Temple in Jerusalem and most of Jerusalem itself has been destroyed and many of the Jews have fled to Alexandria.

Parable Of A Shepherd And One Lost Sheep
(Matthew 18:12-14)

On Repenting And Forgiving
(Matthew 18:15-22)

Then Peter came up and asked him, "Master, how many times can a fellow church member wrong me, and still expect my forgiveness? As many as seven times?"

Jesus answered, "My advice to you is not seven times, but seventy-seven times. If another church member does wrong, go have it out between the two of you privately. If that person listens to you, you have won your brother or sister over. But if that person doesn't listen, take one or two people with you, so that every fact may be supported by two or three witnesses. Then if that one refuses to listen to them, report it to the congregation. If he or she refuses to listen even to the congregation, treat that companion like you would a pagan and toll collector.

"I swear to you, whatever you bind on earth will be considered bound in the heavens, and whatever you release on earth will be considered released in the heavens. Again I assure you, if two of you on earth agree on anything you ask for, it will be done for you by my Father in the heavens. In fact, wherever two or three are gathered together in my name, I will be there among them."

These verses tell us that the Church of Alexandria referred to its members as "brothers and sisters." They did not call themselves

"Christians" until later. This is an early example of a church establishing rules for behavior within the community.

Parable Of A Merciful Ruler And An Unmerciful Underling
(Matthew 18:23-34)

On Castration
(Matthew 19:10-12)

> The disciples said to him, "If that's how it is in the case of a man and his wife, it is better not to marry."
>
> Then he said to them, "Not everyone will be able to accept this advice, only those for whom it was intended. After all, there are castrated men who were born that way, and there are castrated men who were castrated by others, and there are castrated men who castrated themselves because of the Kingdom of Heaven. If you are able to accept this (advice), do so."

This community was very familiar with the tradition of the eunuch, a common phenomenon in the court of Pharaoh for centuries.

Parable Of A Vineyard Owner Hiring And Paying His Workers
(Matthew 20:1-16)

Parable Of Two Sons
(Matthew 21:28-32)

> (He followed that by saying,) "Now what do you think? A man had two sons. He went to the first, and said, 'Son, go and work in the vineyard today.'
>
> He responded, 'I'm your man, sir,' but he didn't move.
>
> Then he went to the second and said the same thing.
>
> He responded, 'I don't want to,' but later on he thought better of it and went (to work).
>
> Which of the two did what the father wanted?"
>
> They said, "The second."

Jesus said to them, "I swear to you, the toll collectors and prostitutes will get into God's kingdom, but you will not. After all, John came to you advocating justice, but you didn't believe him. Yet the toll collectors and prostitutes believed him. Even after you observed (this), you didn't think better of it later and believe him."

They seem to be drawing another distinction between themselves as "new-and-improved-Jews" and the rest of the Jewish population.

Parable Of A Ruler's Wedding Banquet
(Matthew 22:1-14)

Jesus Condemns The Scholars
And Pharisees And Legal Experts
(Matthew 23:1-36)

As he taught the crowd and his disciples, he said, "The scholars and Pharisees occupy the chair of Moses. This means you're supposed to observe and follow everything they tell you. But do not do what they do. After all, they're all talk and no action.

"They invent heavy burdens and lay them on folks' shoulders, but they themselves won't lift a finger to move them. They all do what they do for show. So they widen the little black boxes on their forearms and foreheads and enlarge the tassels on their robes.... They like to be called 'Rabbi' by everyone.

"But you are not to be called 'Rabbi.' After all, you only have one teacher, and all of you belong to the same family. And don't call anyone on earth 'Father,' since you have only one Father, and he is in the heavens. You are not to be called 'Instructors,' because you have only one instructor, the Messiah. Now whoever is greater than you will be your slave. Those who promote themselves will be demoted and those who demote themselves will be promoted.

"But damn you scholars and Pharisees, you phonies! You slam the door of the Kingdom of Heaven in people's faces. You yourselves don't enter, and you block the way of those trying to enter. You scour land and sea to make one convert, and when you do, you make that person more of a child of the Valley of Hinnom than you are.

"Damn you, you blind guides, who say, 'When you swear by the Temple, it doesn't matter, but when you swear by the treasure in the Temple, it is binding.' You blind fools! Which is greater, the treasure or the Temple that makes the treasure sacred? You go on, 'When you swear by the altar, it doesn't matter, but when you swear by the offering that lies on the altar, it is binding.' You sightless souls! Which is greater, the offering or the altar that makes the offering sacred? So when you swear by the altar, you swear by the altar and everything on it. And anyone who swears by the Temple, swears by the Temple and the one who makes it home. And anyone who swears by the heavens swears by the throne of God and the one who occupies it.

"Damn you scholars and Pharisees, you phonies! You pay tithes on mint and dill and cummin, but ignore the really important matters of the Teaching, such as justice and mercy and faith. You should have attended to the last, without ignoring the first. You blind leaders! You strain out a gnat and gulp down a camel!

"Damn you scholars and Pharisees, you phonies! You clean the outside of the cup and plate, but inside they are full of greed and self-indulgence. You blind Pharisees! First clean the inside of the cup so that the outside may be clean as well.

"Damn you scholars and Pharisees, you phonies! You are like painted grave markers. On the outside they look beautiful, but inside they are full of dead bones and every kind of decay. So you too look like decent people on the outside, but on the inside you are doing nothing but posturing and subverting the Teaching.

"Damn you scholars and Pharisees, you phonies! You erect tombs to the prophets and decorate the graves of the righteous, and claim, 'If we had lived in the days of our ancestors, we would not have joined them in spilling the blood of the prophets.' So, you witness against yourselves, that you are descendants of those who murdered the prophets, and you're the spitting image of your ancestors.

"You wriggling mass of baby poisonous snakes! How are you going to escape the sentence to the Valley of Hinnom?

"Therefore I will send you prophets and sages and scholars, some of whom you will kill and crucify, and some you will beat in your synagogues and hound from town to town. As a result there will be on you all the innocent blood shed since the foundation of the earth, from the blood of innocent Abel to the blood of Zechariah, the son of Baruch, whom you murdered between the Temple and the altar. I swear to you, all these things are going to rain down on this generation."

Finally, it all comes out with a vengeance! Wow! The brothers and sisters were really angry at the leaders of the synagogues in Alexandria who had kicked them out of their own synagogues. They needed Jesus to berate them thoroughly.

Indictment Of Jerusalem
(Matthew 23:37-39)

> "Jerusalem, Jerusalem, you murder the prophets and stone those sent to you! How often I wanted to gather your children as a hen (gathers) her own chicks under her wings, but you wouldn't let me. Can't you see, your house is being abandoned? I tell you, you certainly won't see me until you say, 'Blessed is the one who comes in the name of the Lord.'"

In fact, Jerusalem has been virtually abandoned by the time this gospel is written.

The Day Of The Son Of Adam
(Matthew 24:26-28, 37-44)

> "And then if someone says to you, 'Look, here is the Messiah,' or 'Look, there he is!' don't count on it! In fact, if they should say to you, 'Look, he's in the wilderness,' don't go out there; or 'Look, he's in one of the secret rooms,' don't count on it. For just as lightning flashes and lights up the sky from one end to the other, that's what the Son of Adam will be like in his day. Wherever there's a dead body, that's where vultures will congregate.

> "And just as it was in the days of Noah, that's how it will be in the days of the Son of Adam. This is how people behaved then before the flood came. They ate and drank, married and were given in marriage, until the day Noah boarded the Ark, and they were oblivious until the flood came and swept them away. It will be like that on the day the Son of Adam is revealed.

> "There will be two men in the field; one will be taken and the other left. There will be two women grinding meal together; one will be taken and the other left. So stay awake because you don't know on what day your Master is coming.

> "Mark this well! If the homeowner had known when the burglar was coming, he would have been on guard and not have allowed anyone to break into his house. By the same token, you too should be prepared. Remember, the Son of Adam is coming when you least expect it."

Here is more about the "end of the age." The verse about the vultures congregating reflects the Zoroastrian custom of placing corpses on Towers of Silence to be devoured by vultures.

About Being Faithful
(Matthew 24:45-51)

Parable Of Ten Maidens
(Matthew 25:1-13)

Parable Of Money In Trust
(Matthew 25:14-30)

About The Last Judgment
(Matthew 25:31-46)

"When the Son of Adam comes in his glory, accompanied by all his messengers, then he will occupy his glorious throne. Then all peoples will be assembled before him, and he will separate them into groups, much as a shepherd segregates sheep from goats. He will place the sheep to his right and the goats to his left.

"Then the King will say to those at his right , 'Come, you who have the blessing of my Father, inherit the Kingdom prepared for you from the foundation of the world. You may remember, I was hungry and you gave me something to eat. I was thirsty and you gave me something to drink. I was a foreigner and you showed me hospitality. I was naked and you clothed me. I was ill and you visited me. I was in prison and you came to see me.'

"Then the virtuous will say to him, 'Lord, when did we see you hungry and feed you, or thirsty and give you a drink? When did we notice that you were a foreigner and extend hospitality to you? Or naked and clothe you? When did we find you ill or in prison and come to visit you?'

"And the King will answer them, 'I swear to you, whatever you did for the most inconspicuous members of my family, you did for me as well.'

"Next, he will say to those at his left, 'You, damned to the everlasting fire prepared for the Tempter and his messengers, get away from me! You too may remember, I was hungry and you didn't give me anything to eat. I was thirsty and you refused me a drink. I was a foreigner and you failed to extend hospitality to me. Naked and you did not clothe me. Ill and in prison and you did not visit me.'

"Then they will give him a similar reply, 'Lord, when did we notice that you were hungry or thirsty or a foreigner or naked or weak or in prison and did not attempt to help you?'

"Then he will answer them, 'I swear to you, whatever you didn't do for the most inconspicuous member of my family, you did not do for me.'

"The second group will then head for everlasting punishment, but the virtuous for everlasting life."

This famous passage recreates the Zoroastrian belief that those who live moral and virtuous lives will inherit Paradise while those who live immoral lives, void of compassion, will inherit punishment. In Persian theology, the punishment only lasts until the final battle between the forces of good and evil, after which those who have been punished are joined with the righteous in eternal bliss on a cleansed Earth. For these Alexandrians, punishment is everlasting with no possibility of parole.

Judas Commits Suicide
(Matthew 27:3-10)

Then Judas, who had turned him in, realizing that he had been condemned, was overcome with remorse and returned the month's wages to the ranking priests and elders with this remark, "I have made a grave mistake in turning this innocent man in."

But they said, "What's that to us? That's your problem!"

And hurling the money into the Temple he slipped away, and went out and hanged himself.

The ranking priests took the coins and said, "It wouldn't be right to put this back into the Temple treasury, since now it's blood money."

So they devised a plan and bought the Potter's Field as a burial ground for foreigners. As a result, that field has been known as "the Bloody Field" even to this day. So the prediction Jeremiah the prophet made came true:

And they took the thirty silver coins,
the price put on a man's head
– this is exactly the price they put on him among the Israelites –
and they donated it for the Potter's Field,
as my Lord commanded me.

68

Judas commits suicide only in Matthew, not in Mark or Luke. There is some knowledge in the Jewish community in Alexandria of "the Bloody Field," where the dead bodies of poor people were dumped without burial. And notice the fresh quote from Jeremiah. This is the 21st new quote from the Septuagint in this gospel.

Crucifixion Events
(Matthew 27:51-53)

> The earth quaked, rocks were split apart, and the tombs were opened, and many bodies of sleeping saints came back to life. And they came out of the tombs after his resurrection and went into the Holy City, where they appeared to many.

Only in Egypt would people think of such a thing! And they were big on earthquakes!

Guarding The Tomb
(Matthew 27:62-66)

> On the next day, which is the day after Preparation, the ranking priests and the Pharisees met with Pilate and said, "Your Excellency, we remember what that imposter said while he was still alive: 'After three days I am going to be raised up.' So order the tomb sealed for three days so his disciples won't come and steal his body, and tell everyone, 'He has been raised from the dead,' in which case, the last deception will be worse than the first."
>
> Pilate said to them, "You have a guard! Go and secure it the best way you know how." So they went and secured the tomb by sealing (it with a) stone and posting a guard.

Those damned Pharisees are at it again!

The Resurrection
(Matthew 28:2-4, 9-10)

> (Before dawn on Sunday), there was a strong earthquake. You see, a messenger of the Lord had come down from the sky, arrived (at the tomb), rolled away the stone, and sat on it. The messenger gave off a dazzling light and wore clothes as white as snow. Now those who kept watch were paralyzed with fear and looked like corpses themselves.

Then, Jesus met (the two Marys) and said, "Hello!" And they came up and took hold of his feet and paid him homage. He said to them, "Don't be afraid. Go tell my companions so they can leave for Galilee, where they will see me.

First written story of a physical appearance by Jesus immediately following the resurrection.

Bribing The Soldiers
(Matthew 28:11-15)

While (the women) were on their way (to tell the disciples), some of the guards returned to the city and reported to the ranking priests everything that had happened. They met with the elders and hatched a plan. They bribed the soldiers with an adequate amount of money and ordered them: "Tell everybody that his disciples came at night and stole his body while we were asleep. If the Governor should hear about this, we will deal with him. You need have no worries." So they took the money and did as they had been instructed. And this story has been passed around among the Jews until this very day.

Especially the Jews in Alexandria

Jesus Encourages The Disciples In Galilee
(Matthew 28:16-20)

Then the eleven disciples went to the mountain in Galilee when Jesus had told them to go. When they saw him they paid him homage, but some were dubious. And Jesus approached them and spoke these words: "All authority has been given to me in heaven and on earth. You are to go and make followers of all peoples. You are to baptize them in the name of the Father, and the Son, and the sacred breath of life. Teach them to observe everything I commanded. I will be with you day in and day out, as you will see, so long as this world continues its course."

Notice that there is no ascension here. The text assumes that Jesus will continue to live a physical life in the presence of the disciples to the "end of the age."

Conclusion

It has been whispered in academic circles that Jesus is not divine in Matthew, but not too many have said that out loud. This is the blockbuster piece in this chapter. If the assumption is correct that the Jewish Jesus followers in Alexandria wrote this gospel, it makes sense that they would have to consider Jesus wholly human, as did James, Jesus' brother, and Peter, Jesus' best friend. "You shall have no gods other than me" (Exodus 20:3) was taken very seriously in the early Alexandrian church.

Also, the contrast between the "Empire of God" in Mark and the "Kingdom of Heaven" in Matthew is very significant in this chapter. The Empire is temporal and the Kingdom is celestial. The Empire is tomorrow and the Kingdom is later. In Rome there is a desperate need for Jesus to come again. In Alexandria there is no need to rush the debut of the Kingdom. Mark and Matthew are as much different as they are alike.

Chapter 6
Luke is the Gentile Gospel of Antioch, Written by a Woman Scribe

The Gospel of Luke is the gospel of the Gentile "Christian" community in Antioch, Syria. It is their corporate expression of faith, written around 78-80 CE by a very literate scribe and dedicated to Luke, the physician friend of Paul. Physicians in these days were men with the sharpest knives, a jar of leeches, and a basket of herbs. They did not go to medical school and were mostly illiterate. Luke was not an obstetrician/gynecologist.

The Gospel dedicated to Luke presents the actions and sayings of Jesus as the human-then-divine Savior, who was as much committed to social justice as religious reform. The Antiochian Church is a sophisticated Greek-thinking community which believed that Jesus' mission is to and for all the inhabitants of the Earth, and they say that by (a) indicating that women have a new place of importance among the disciples of Jesus; (b) tracing his genealogy back to Adam, rather than Abraham; (c) including stories that commend members of a despised race, the Samaritans; and (d) promising that Gentiles would have an opportunity to accept Jesus as Savior. This is Paul's home church. He is their hero, and this is seen in their writing of the Acts of the Apostles, also.

The Gospel dedicated to Luke may tell us more about the people of the church of Antioch, their needs and hopes, than it tells us about the historical Jesus. They needed Jesus to be a lot like the Paul that they remembered from twenty years before, a traveling Jewish preacher who was as passionate about the salvation of Gentiles as the salvation of Jews. They hoped that Jesus had instituted the Kingdom of God in their present time as well as in the afterlife. For that purpose, they needed Jesus to be a social reformer as well as a religious reformer, promoting justice and fairness and peace among all peoples. It was important to them that Jesus be born human, live and die as a human, but be resurrected as a god who ascended to God the Father in heaven.

The Roman Gospel dedicated to Mark sailed over from Rome and constitutes 60% of Luke. The Jewish-Egyptian Gospel dedicated to Matthew sailed over from Alexandria, and the new material original in Matthew constitutes 20% of Luke. Most of the original material in Luke is found in the section dealing with the journey to Jerusalem. Thus, Luke is the fourth tier of the Synoptic Gospel wedding cake since Luke is built primarily on Matthew, which is built on Mark, which is based on Paul's theology. There are twenty-four chapters in Luke, four less than in Matthew, but there are some very long chapters in Luke.

There are no known copies of this gospel that were made before the middle of the fourth century. The scribe of the Church of Antioch was probably a well-educated, highly intelligent Greek poetess, based on information presented in Chapter 8. The gospel was written in twelfth-grade Greek.

The concept of Jesus presented in this gospel differs from the concepts in Mark and Matthew. In Mark, Jesus is the powerful god who will soon make a triumphal entry into Rome as the emperor of the Empire of God. In Matthew, Jesus is the human messiah who teaches how to attain life in the Kingdom of Heaven. In Luke, Jesus is born as a human, serves as a great social and religious reformer in the Kingdom of God and is made a god through his resurrection, after which he ascends to heaven.

The church of Antioch knew little about the geography of the Galilee, Samaria and Judea, even though it was the closest to that area of the three synoptic gospel churches. This is seen in the narrative when Jesus pops up in various wide-spread places in much less time than it takes to travel there. The Antiochians were also unaware of some social situations in the country to their south. They assumed there are "inns" in Bethlehem and Jericho since there were inns in Antioch. Poverty and middle eastern hospitality rules precluded inns in Bethlehem and Jericho.

The church of Antioch reflected its environment: physical, historical, demographic, philosophical and theological. Geographically, Antioch was situated on the Orontes River, seven miles from where it empties into the northeast corner of the Mediterranean. Its acropolis and citadel were on the side of Mt. Silpius, which dominated the city's eastern side. It was the capital of the Roman province of Syria and boasted of many outstanding buildings, including a sprawling palace on the island in the middle of the river. There was the usual circus for chariot races and the theater and amphitheater for other amusements. The city was located at the intersection of two major overland trade routes and also benefitted from shipping commerce from the Mediterranean.

The city was founded in 300 BCE by Seleucus Nicator, who named it after his father, Antiochus. The Seleucid dynasty was to Syria what the Ptolemy dynasty was to Egypt, both being descendants of generals of Alexander the Great who divided up Alexander's Empire after his death. Antioch was conquered by the Romans in 64 BCE, and they made it a provincial capital. During the first Jewish war in 66-73 CE (during which time the Temple in Jerusalem was destroyed), there were anti-Jewish riots in Antioch. It appears that there were few if any Jews in the Church of Antioch, and that the gospel reflects anti-Jewish tendencies, even though Paul, a Jew, is their favorite son.

At the time Luke was written, Antioch was the third largest city in the Roman Empire, a center of Greek culture and a business center. With just under nine hundred thousand inhabitants, every ethnic group in the region was represented. Syrians were in the majority. Jews had lived in the city since it was founded, but not in great numbers as in Alexandria. There were Romans, Greeks, Persians, Parthians and a goodly number from Asia Minor, all living together rather peacefully and represented on the city council of elders. They enjoyed a prosperous urban culture.

The first-century Antiochians were very Greek in their approach to things philosophical. Dualism dominated their thought world. Compassion and the compassionate use of money was the most valued currency in the Church of Antioch. Antioch was at the crossroads of religious thought. From the south came Egyptian and Jewish religions. From the east came Zoroastrianism. From the west came Gnosticism, Greek mystery religions and Roman emperor worship. They heard stories about gods who became human and humans who became gods, including Augustus Caesar who was born of a virgin and made a god at his death.

Conclusion

Again, it has been whispered about that the scribe of the Gospel dedicated to Luke was a woman. If a poetess were indeed the scribe, then Luke and Acts are the only two "books" of the New Testament penned by a woman. The case for her authorship is presented in the next two chapters.

A significant part of the theory put forth in this book is that the Synoptic Gospels were written in sequence as Mark, Matthew and Luke. The case for that is strengthened by the appearance in Luke of two compromises the scribe made between Mark and Matthew. First, she presented a human Jesus, as per Matthew, who became divine at his resurrection, as Jesus is divine throughout Mark. Secondly, she took the "Empire of God" from Mark and the "Kingdom of Heaven" from Matthew and created the "Kingdom of God" which has begun on earth and will continue later in heaven.

Chapter 7
Roman and Alexandrian Gospels
Make an Impact on Antioch

It is clear that the Roman Gospel dedicated to Mark was available to the Church of Antioch as they wrote their gospel, since 60% of Luke is made up of material that originated in Mark. The scribe of Antioch took the liberty of editing, rephrasing and repositioning the text of Mark, as well as improving the quality of the Greek.

The Church of Antioch also had a copy of the Jewish-Egyptian Gospel dedicated to Matthew available as the scribe devised this church's gospel. Many scholars believe that Matthew and Luke were written simultaneously, and that both churches used a hypothetical document called "Q."

"Q" stands for the German word *quelle*, which means "source." Some scholars believe "Q" was a written work. Others think it was commonly known oral tradition. The existence of such a document cannot be proven, so that is another theory. The definition of "Q" is material that is common to both Matthew and Luke but is not found in Mark. Rather than postulating the existence of another document of which there are no copies yet discovered, a part of this theory simply says that Matthew was written first, and Antioch used material from Matthew just as Antioch used material from Mark.

The poetess/scribe of Antioch sometimes quotes from Matthew verbatim and sometimes adapts the language of Matthew to suit her own purposes, just as she does with Mark. There are a number of books available which contain comparison columns of this material common to

Matthew and Luke, the best of which is *The Complete Gospels*, edited by Robert J. Miller, (Polebridge Press,1994).

The following is a merging of this common material. It is included to show the reader the 20% of the Antiochian Gospel that is dependent on material from the Alexandrian Gospel. None of the following passages is from the Roman Gospel. Only two or three of these passages are narrative in nature. The bulk of the verses are sayings, the first one by John the Baptist and the rest by Jesus. The verses that are italicized have been added in Luke to the Alexandrian material. These passages are in the order in which they appear in Luke.

John's Pronouncement
(Luke 3:7-9, 16-17; Matthew 3:7-12)

> But when he saw that many of the Pharisees and Sadducees were coming for baptism, he said, "You wriggling mass of baby poisonous snakes! Who warned you to flee from the impending doom? Well then, start producing fruit suitable for a change of heart, and don't even think of saying to yourselves, 'We have Abraham as our father.' Let me tell you, God can raise up children for Abraham right out of these rocks. Even now the axe is aimed at the root of the trees. Every tree therefore that does not produce good fruit is cut down and thrown into the fire.

> "Someone more powerful than I will succeed me, whose sandal straps I am not fit to bend down and untie. I baptize you with water to signal a change of heart, but he will baptize you with the sacred breath of life and with fire. His pitchfork is in his hand, to make a clean sweep of his threshing floor, and to gather the wheat into his granary, but the chaff he will burn with unquenchable fire."

This first passage was copied virtually verbatim from Matthew. After this, she puts her own spin on virtually all the rest of the passages from Matthew.

Jesus' Temptation And Profession Of Faith
(Luke 4:1-13; Matthew 4:1-11)

> Then Jesus, full of the sacred breath of life, left the Jordan and was guided by the breath of life into the Wilderness, to be tempted by the Tempter for forty days and forty nights. He ate nothing during that time. He was very hungry.

(1) The Tempter said, "If you are God's son, order these stones to turn into bread."

Jesus answered him, "It is written, 'One is not to live on bread alone, but on every word that comes from the mouth of God.'"

(2) Then the Tempter took him to the Holy City, and set him on the highest point (of the wall around) the Temple area, and said to him, "If you are God's son, jump off; remember, it is written, 'He will give orders about you to his messengers,' and 'With their hands they will catch you, so that you will not even stub your toe on a stone.'"

Jesus said, "Elsewhere it is written, 'Do not put the Lord your God to the test.'"

(3) Again, the Tempter took him to a very high mountain, and showed him all the kingdoms of the world and their splendor, and said to him, "I will give you authority over all this and the glory that comes with it. Understand, it has been handed over to me, and I can give it to anyone I want. So, if you will kneel down and pay homage to me, I will give you all this."

Finally Jesus said to him, "Get out of here, Tempter! Remember, it is written, 'You are to pay homage to the Lord your God, and you are to serve him alone.'"

When the Tempter had tried every kind of temptation, he let him alone for the time being. Then messengers from the heavens arrived out of nowhere and looked after Jesus.

The scribe of Luke reversed the order of the second and third temptation as presented in Matthew, for no apparent reason.

Blessings And Condemnations:
(Luke 6:20-26; Matthew 5:1-12)

Facing the crowd (up on the steep hillside), he sat down and began to speak, and this is what he spoke to them:

Blessed are the poor in the breath of life,
for the Kingdom of Heaven belongs to them.
But damn you who are rich,
for you have received your consolation.
Blessed are those who mourn, for they will be comforted.
Blessed are those who weep now, for they will laugh.
But damn you who are laughing now, for you will mourn and weep.

Blessed are the gentle, for they will inherit the earth.
Blessed are those who hunger and thirst for justice,
for they will have a feast.
But damn you who are full now, for you will be hungry.
Blessed are the merciful, for they will receive mercy.
Blessed are those with undefiled hearts, for they will see God.
Blessed are the peacemakers,
for they will be known as children of God.
Blessed are those who have suffered persecution
for the sake of justice,
for the Kingdom of Heaven belongs to them.
Blessed are you when people hate you,
and exclude you and revile you
and persecute you and spread malicious gossip
about you because of me.
Rejoice and be glad! Your compensation is great in the heavens.
Remember that this is how they
persecuted the prophets who preceded you.
But damn you, when all speak well of you,
for that is what their ancestors did to the phony prophets.

In Luke, "poor in the breath of life" is shortened to "poor"; "those who hunger and thirst for justice" is shortened to "those who hunger." In both cases, this reflects Antioch's concern for the needy. The scribe also adds the curses to the Alexandrian blessings.

Deeper Spirituality And Reverse Payback
(Luke 6:29-31; Matthew 5:38-42; Matthew 7:12)

"You know that our ancestors were told, 'An eye for an eye' and 'A tooth for a tooth.' But I say to you: Do not react violently against the one who is evil. When someone slaps you on the right cheek, turn the other as well. When someone wants to sue you for your undergarment, let that person have your outer garment along with it. Further, when anyone conscripts you for one mile, go an extra mile. Give to the one who begs from you, and do not turn away the one who tries to borrow from you. *And if anyone takes away your belongings, do not ask for them back.* Treat people the way you want them to treat you, for that is the theme of all the Teaching and the Prophets.

This addition speaks for itself.

Deeper Spirituality And Love Of Enemies
(Luke 6:27-28, 32-36; Matthew 5:43-48)

"You know we once were told, 'You shall love your neighbor' and 'You shall hate your enemy.' But I say to you: Love your enemies. Do favors for those who hate you. Bless those who curse you. Pray for those who abuse and persecute you. You will then become children of your Father in the heavens, who makes the sun rise on the bad and the good, and sends rain on the just and the unjust. Tell me, if you love those who love you, why should you be commended for that? Even toll collectors love those who love them. If you greet only your friends, and do favors only for those who do favors for you, what have you done that is exceptional? Even the Gentiles (Matthew) or *sinners* (Luke) do as much, don't they? *If you lend to those from whom you hope to gain, why should you be commended for that? Even sinners lend to sinners, in order to get as much in return.*

"But love your enemies, and do them favors, and lend, expecting nothing in return. Your reward will be great, and you will be children of the Most High. As you know, he is generous to the ungrateful and the wicked. Always be compassionate in the way your Father is always compassionate."

The Jewish church of Alexandria casts dispersion on Gentiles, but the scribe of the Gentile church of Antioch changes the word "Gentile" to "sinners." This appears to support the theory that Antioch used a copy of Matthew, rather than "Q." If Antioch and Alexandria had used the same source document, why did they choose different words here? The point in the added verses in Luke is the emphasis on compassion and social justice.

Deeper Spirituality And Fairness
(Luke 6:37-38, 41-42; Matthew 7:1-5)

"Don't pass judgment, and you will not be judged. Don't condemn, and you will not be condemned. *Forgive and you will be forgiven. Give, and it will be given to you. They will put in your lap a full measure, packed down, sifted, and overflowing.* Don't forget, the judgment you hand out will be the judgment you get back. And the standard you apply will be the standard applied to you, and then some.

"Why do you notice the sliver in your friend's eye, but overlook the timber in your own? How can you say to your friend, 'Friend, let me get the sliver out of your eye,' when you don't notice the timber in your own eye? You phony, first take the timber out of your own eye, and then you will see well enough to remove the sliver from your friend's eye.

The emphasis on the compassionate use of money is the cause of this addition.

On Discernment
(Luke 6:43-45; Matthew 7:15-20; Matthew 12:35)

> "Be on the lookout for phony prophets, who make their pitch disguised as sheep. Inside they are really voracious wolves. You will know who they are by what they produce. Since when do people pick grapes from thorn bushes, or figs from thistles?

> "Every healthy tree produces choice fruit, but the diseased tree produces rotten fruit. Each tree is known by its own fruit. A healthy tree cannot produce rotten fruit, nor can a diseased tree produce choice fruit. Every tree that does not produce choice fruit is cut down and thrown into the fire.

> "The good person produces good from the fund of good in the heart, and the evil person produces evil from the evil within. *After all, out of the surplus of the heart the mouth speaks.* Remember, you will know who they are by what they produce.

The verse about "phony prophets" and the verse about being "cut down and thrown into the fire" are omitted in Luke, and the one verse is added.

On Importance Of Building One's Theology Carefully
(Luke 6:47-49; Matthew 7:24-27)

> "Everyone who follows me and pays attention to these words of mine and acts on them, I will show you what it is like. That person is like a shrewd builder erecting a house, who dug deeply, and laid the foundation upon bedrock. Later the rain fell, and the river burst against the house, and the winds blew and pounded that house, yet it did not collapse, because its foundation rested on bedrock.

> "Everyone who listens to these words of mine and does not act on them will be like a careless builder, who erected a house on the sand without a foundation. When the rain fell, and the river burst against the house, and the winds blew and pounded that house, it collapsed quickly. The collapse of that house was a disaster."

This saying is quoted from Matthew and the meaning is the same, but the Greek has been upgraded.

Jesus Cures A Roman Officer's Slave
(Luke 7:1-10; Luke 13:28-30; Matthew 8:5-13)

> When he finished preaching to the people, he went back to Capernaum. A Roman officer (in town) had a slave he was very fond of, who was sick and about to die. *When he heard about Jesus, he sent some Jewish elders to him to ask him to come and cure his slave. When they came to Jesus, they pleaded with him urgently, saying, "He deserves to have you do this for him. As you know, he loves our people, and even built a synagogue for us."*

> Jesus said, "I will go and cure (his slave)," and he went with them. When he was not far from the house, the Roman officer sent friends to him, saying to him, "Do not trouble yourself, sir, for I don't deserve to have you in my house. That's why I did not presume to come to you in person. Just say the word, and let my boy be cured. After all, I myself am under orders, with soldiers under me. I order one to go and he goes. I order another to come and he comes. And (I order) my slave to do something and he does it."

> When Jesus heard this he was amazed at him, and turned and said to the crowd that followed him, "Let me tell you, I have not found such faith in a single Israelite! I predict that many will come from east and west, and from north and south, and dine with Abraham, Isaac, and Jacob in the Kingdom of Heaven, while those who think the Kingdom belongs to them will be thrown where it is utterly dark. There will be weeping and grinding of teeth out there. *And remember, those who will be first are last, and those who will be last are first."*

> Jesus said, "Be on your way. (His) trust will be the measure of the results." When the emissaries returned to the house, they found that the servant had been cured at the precise moment (that Jesus spoke those words).

This is one of the few narrative passages found in this common material. The scribe of Antioch adds words in two places to improve the story.

A Question From John The Baptist
(Luke 7:18-23; Matthew 11:2-6)

> (After the disciples left, Jesus) moved on from there to teach and proclaim in the towns (of Galilee).

The disciples of John brought reports to (John) in prison of all these things the Messiah was doing. John summoned two of his disciples and sent them to the Lord to ask, "Are you the one who is to come, or shall we to wait for another?"

When these men came to Jesus, they said, "John the Baptist sent us to you to ask, 'Are you the one who is to come, or shall we wait for another?'"

Jesus had just cured many of their diseases and plagues and evil spirits, and restored sight to many who were blind. He answered them, "Go report to John what you have seen and heard:

> the blind see again,
> the lame walk,
> lepers are cleansed
> the deaf hear,
> the dead are raised,
> and the poor have the good news preached to them.
> Blessed are those who don't take offense at me."

While the rest of this passage is copied virtually verbatim, the scribe adds a couple of sentences to make clearer what is happening.

Jesus Pays Tribute To John The Baptist
(Luke 7:24-35; Luke 16:16; Matthew 11:7-19)

After John's disciples had gone, Jesus began to talk about John to the crowds: "What did you go out to the wilderness to gawk at? A reed shaking in the wind? What did you really go out to see? A man dressed in fancy clothes? But wait! Those who dress fashionably *and live in luxury* are found in palaces. Come on, what did you go out to see? A prophet? Yes, that's what you went out to see, yet someone more than a prophet. This is the one of whom it was written,

> Here is my messenger,
> Whom I send on ahead of you
> to prepare your way before you.

I tell you, among those born of women none is greater than John the Baptist. Yet, the least in the Kingdom of Heaven is greater than he.

All the people, even the toll collectors, who were listening and had been baptized by John, vindicated God's plan. But the Pharisees and the legal experts, who had not be baptized by him, rejected the purpose of God for themselves.

The Teaching and the Prophets were in effect until John came. Since John arrived, the Kingdom of Heaven has been breaking in violently. The Kingdom has been proclaimed as good news and violent people are attempting to break into it violently. But it is easier for the world to disappear than for one tiny piece of the Teaching to drop out.

You see, the Prophets and even the Teaching predicted everything that was to happen prior to John's time. And if you are willing to admit it, John is the Elijah who was expected. Anyone here with two ears had better listen!

What do the people of this generation remind me of? They are like children sitting in the marketplaces who call out to others:

> We played the flute for you, but you would not dance.
> We sang a dirge but you would not mourn.

Just remember, John the Baptist appeared on the scene, eating no bread and drinking no wine, and they say, 'He is demented.' The Son of Adam appeared on the scene both eating and drinking; and they say, 'There is a glutton and a drunk, a crony of toll collectors and sinners!' Indeed, wisdom is vindicated by all her children."

Another minor addition

Nature Of Discipleship
(Luke 9:57-62; Matthew 8:19-22)

As Jesus was going down the road, a scholar came up and said to him, "Teacher, I will follow you wherever you go."

Jesus said to him, "Foxes have dens, and birds of the sky have nests, but the Son of Adam has nowhere to rest his head."

To another he said, "Follow me."

But he said, "Master, first let me go and bury my father."

Jesus said, "Leave it to the dead to bury their own dead. *But you, follow me and go out and announce the Kingdom of God.*"

Another said, "I will follow you, sir; but let me first say good-bye to my people at home."

Jesus said to him, "No one who puts his hand to the plow and looks back is qualified for the Kingdom of God."

The third point has been added.

Condemnation Of Galilean Towns
(Luke 10:13-15; Matthew 11:20-24)

Then Jesus began to condemn the towns where he had performed most of his miracles, because they had not changed their ways: "Damn you, Chorazin! Damn you, Bethsaida! If the miracles done in you had been done in Tyre and Sidon, they would have changed their ways long ago, and (would have sat) in sackcloth and ashes. So I tell you, Tyre and Sidon will be better off at the Judgment than you. And you, Capernaum, you don't think you will be exalted to the heavens, do you? No, you will go to Hell! Because if the miracles done among you had been done in Sodom, it would still be around. So I tell you, the land of Sodom will be better off at the Judgment than you."

The Antiochian scribe quotes verbatim from "Damn you" to "go to Hell." The rest is omitted.

Model Prayer
(Luke 11:2-4; Matthew 6:9-13)

"When you pray, say:

Our Father in the heavens,
your name be revered.
Impose your Kingdom,
enact your will on earth,
as you have in the heavens.
Provide us with the bread
we need day by day.
Forgive our debts
to the extent we have forgiven
everyone in debt to us.
And please don't subject us to test after test,
but rescue us from evil.

"Enact your will on earth, as you have in the heavens" and "rescue us from evil" are not repeated in Luke.

Teaching About The Return Of Unclean Spirits
(Luke 11:24-26; Matthew 12:43-45)

When an unclean spirit leaves a person, it wanders through waterless places in search of a resting place. When it doesn't find one, it then says, 'I will return to the home I left.' It then returns and finds it empty, swept and refurbished. Next, it goes out and brings back with it seven other spirits more vile than itself, who enter and settle in there. So that person ends up worse off than when he or she started. That's how it will be for this perverse generation."

Verbatim copy of Matthew except for the last sentence, which is in Matthew, only

Teaching That The Eye Is The Light Of The Body
(Luke 11:34-36; Matthew 6:22-23)

Your eye is the body's lamp. When your eye is clear, your whole body is flooded with light. When your eye is clouded, your body is shrouded in darkness. Take care, then, that the light within you is not darkness. If the light within you is darkness, how dark that can be! *If then your whole body is flooded with light, and no corner of it is darkness, it will be completely illuminated as when a lamp's rays engulf you.*

Another minor addition

Eating With Pharisees
(Luke 11:37-41; Matthew 23:25-26)

While Jesus was speaking, a Pharisee invited him to dinner at his house. So he came and reclined at the table. The Pharisee was astonished to see that he did not first wash before dinner.

But the Lord said to him, "Damn you scribes and Pharisees, you phonies! You clean the outside of cups and dishes, but inside you are full of greed and evil. You blind fools! First clean the inside of the cup (and the plate), then the outside will be clean too. *Did not the one who made the outside also make the inside? Still, donate what is inside to charity, and then you'll see how everything comes clean for you.*"

The scribe took a passage from Matthew, gave it a narrative context and then added words about the compassionate use of one's possessions.

Deeper Spirituality And Living Life In The Present
(Luke 12:22-31, 33-34; Matthew 6:19-21, 25-34)

"So I tell you, don't fret about your life, what you are going to eat and drink, or about your body, what you are going to wear. There is more to living than food and clothing. Look at the birds of the air. They don't plant or harvest or gather into silo or barn. Yet your Father in the heavens feeds them. You are worth more than the birds, aren't you? Can any of you add one hour to life by fretting about it?

"So if you are not able to do a small thing like that, why worry about the rest, including your clothes? Notice how the wild lilies grow. They don't slave and they never spin. Yet let me tell you, even Solomon at the height of his glory was never decked out like one of them. If God dresses up the grass in the field, which is here today and tomorrow is thrown in the oven, will he not care for you even more, you who don't take anything for granted? Therefore, do not fret. Do not say, 'What am I going to eat?' or 'What am I going to drink?' or 'What am I going to wear?'

"These are all things **Gentiles** (Matthew) or *nations of the world* (Luke) seek. After all, your Father in the heavens is aware that you need them. Instead, seek (God's) Kingdom and his justice first, and all these things will come to you as a bonus. So, do not fret about tomorrow. Let tomorrow fret about itself. The troubles that today brings are enough.

"Do not acquire possessions here on earth, where moth or insect eats away and where robbers break in and steal. Sell your possessions, and donate to charity. Make yourselves purses that don't wear out, with inexhaustible wealth in the heavens, where neither moth nor insect eats away and where robbers do not break in and steal. As you know, what you treasure is your heart's true measure.

This is the second instance where the scribe of Antioch refused to accept the insult from Alexandria. The Greek word used in Matthew can mean "Gentile" or "pagan" or "heathen." All of these meanings imply a "non-believer." The Gentile Church of Antioch used the word "Gentile" to mean "non-Jewish," but they certainly did not think of themselves as pagans or heathens. The scribe's words in Greek imply that most people in the Roman Empire at this time were not Christians. If there had been a "Q" document, what would it have said at this point?

About Being Faithful
(Luke 12:35-48; Matthew 24:43-51)

Keep your belts fastened and your lamps lighted. Imitate those who are waiting for their master to come home from a wedding, ready to open the door for him as soon as he arrives and knocks. Blessed are those slaves the master finds alert when he arrives. I swear to you, he will put on an apron, have them recline at the table, and proceed to wait on them. If he gets home around midnight, or even around three o'clock in the morning, and finds them so, blessed are those slaves!

Mark this well! If the homeowner had known when the burglar was coming, he would have been on guard and not have allowed anyone to break into his house. By the same token, you too should be prepared. Remember, the Son of Adam is coming when you least expect it."

Peter said, "Lord, are you telling this parable just for us or for the benefit of everyone?"

The Lord said, "Who then is the reliable and shrewd manager to whom the master assigns responsibility for his household staff, to dole out to the other slaves their food allowance at the right time? Blessed is the slave who's on the job when his master arrives. I swear to you that he will put him in charge of all his property. But suppose that worthless slave says to himself, 'My master is taking his time getting here,' and begins to beat the servants and the maids, and to eat and drink and get drunk with drunkards. That slave's master will show up on the day he least expects and at an hour he doesn't suspect. He will cut him to pieces, and assign him a fate fit for the phonies and the faithless. (Those who share this fate) will moan and grind their teeth.

And the slave who knew what his master wanted, but didn't get things ready or act properly, will be flogged severely. On the other hand, the slave who didn't know what his master wanted, yet did things that deserve punishment, will be flogged lightly. A great deal will be required of everyone to whom much is given. Yet even more will be demanded from the one to whom a great deal has been entrusted.

There is a preface and a postscript added to this piece from Matthew, as well as an unanswered question from Peter. The rest is verbatim, except the scribe of Antioch doesn't like that phrase about moaning and grinding teeth, using it only once, compared to several times in Matthew.

Settling With One's Accuser
(Luke 12:57-59; Matthew 5:25-26)

"Why can you not decide for yourselves what is right? When you are about to appear with your accuser before the magistrate, do your best to settle with him on the way, or else your accuser might drag

you up before the judge, and the judge turn you over to the jailer, and the jailer throw you in prison. I tell you, you will never get out of there till you have paid the last red cent.

A minor addition

Parable Of Yeast Hidden In A Large Amount Of Bread Dough
(Luke 13:21; Matthew 13:33)

> The Kingdom of Heaven (Matthew) or *Kingdom of God* (Luke) is like leaven which a woman took and concealed in fifty pounds of flour until it was all leavened.

Which way would it have read in a "Q" document? This points to the difference between the idea of the Kingdom of Heaven in Alexandria, which was a future kingdom up there and out there, and the Kingdom of God in Antioch, which was a present kingdom here and now as well as a future kingdom at the end of time.

On Salvation
(Luke 13:22-30; Matthew 7:13-14, 21-23)

> *On his journey, he passed through towns and villages, teaching and making his way toward Jerusalem. And someone asked him, "Sir, is it true that only a few are going to be saved?"*
>
> Jesus answered, "Try to get in through the narrow gate. Wide and smooth is the road that leads to destruction. The majority are taking that route. Narrow and rough is the way that leads to life. Only a minority discover it. A majority will try to get in and will not be able.
>
> Not everyone who addresses me as 'Master, Master,' shall enter the Kingdom of Heaven, only those who carry out the will of my Father in the heavens. *Once the master of the house gets up and bars the door, you'll be left standing outside and knocking at the door, saying, 'Sir, open up for us.'*
>
> On that day many will address me: 'Master, Master, did we not use your name when we prophesied? Or when we exorcized demons? Or when we performed all those miracles? *We ate and drank with you, and you taught in our streets.'* Then I will tell them honestly, 'I do not know where you come from. Get away from me, you subverters of the Teaching!'
>
> And there will be weeping and grinding teeth out there when (they) see Abraham and Isaac and Jacob and all the prophets in the

Kingdom of God and (them)selves thrown out. And people will come from east and west, from north and south, and dine in the Kingdom of God."

This passage is a duke's mixture of material taken from various places in Matthew, plus new material.

Indictment Of Jerusalem
(Luke 13:34-35; Matthew 23:37-39)

Jerusalem, Jerusalem, you murder the prophets and stone those sent to you! How often I wanted to gather your children as a hen (gathers) her own chicks under her wings, but you wouldn't let me. Can't you see, your house is being abandoned? I tell you, you certainly won't see me until the time comes when you say, 'Blessed is the one who comes in the name of the Lord.'"

Almost an exact quote from Matthew

Parable Of A Ruler's Wedding Banquet
(Luke 14:15-24; Matthew 22:1-10)

When one of his fellow guests heard this, he said to him, "Blessed are those who will eat bread in the Kingdom of God!"

Jesus told them a second parable: "The Kingdom of Heaven is like a ruler who threw a wedding banquet for his son, and invited many guests. At the dinner hour the host sent his slaves to tell those who were invited to the wedding banquet, *'Come, it's ready now.'* But they would not come.

And one by one they all began to make excuses. The first said to him, 'I just bought a farm, and I have to go and inspect it. Please excuse me.' And another said, 'I just bought five pairs of oxen, and I'm on my way to check them out. Please excuse me.' And another said, 'I just got married, and so I cannot attend.'

So the slave came back and reported these (excuses) to his master. Then he sent additional slaves with the instructions: 'Tell those invited,

"Look, the banquet is ready, the oxen and fat calves have been slaughtered, and everything is set. Come to the wedding!"'

But they were unconcerned and went off, one to his own farm, one to (take care of) his business, while the rest seized his servants, attacked and killed them.

Now the ruler got angry and sent his armies to destroy those murderers and burn their city. Then he told his slaves, 'The wedding celebration is ready, but those we have invited didn't prove deserving. *Go out quickly to the town gates and into the streets and lanes of the town, and invite anybody you find to the wedding, and bring in the poor and crippled and blind and lame.'*

One slave (came back and) said, 'Sir, your orders have been carried out, and there's still room.'

The master said to the slave, 'Then go out into the roads and the country lanes, and force people to come in so my house may be filled. Believe you me, not one of those who were given invitations shall taste my banquet.'

And those slaves went out into the streets and collected everybody they could find, the bad and good alike. And the wedding hall was filled with guests.

The additions are to dress up the story and stress the themes of social justice and compassionate treatment of the needy.

Parable Of A Shepherd And One Lost Sheep

(Luke 15:3-7; Matthew 18:12-14)

So he told them this parable: "What do you think of this? Is there any one of you who owns a hundred sheep and one of them gets lost, who wouldn't leave the ninety-nine on the hillsides in the wilderness, and go after the one that got lost until he finds it? And when he finds it, *he lifts it upon his shoulders*, happier over finding the one than over the ninety-nine that never got lost. *Once he gets home, he invites his friends and his neighbors over, and says to them, 'Celebrate with me, because I have found my lost sheep.'*

I'm telling you it will be just like this in the heavens. There will be more celebrating over one sinner who has a change of heart than over ninety-nine virtuous people who have no need to change their hearts. And so it is the intention of your Father in the heavens that not one of these souls be lost.

An expansion of the parable

Conclusion

Again, the point of presenting this material in this chapter is to show the passages that are common to the Alexandrian and Antiochian

Gospels, that the scribe of Antioch used from the Jewish-Egyptian Gospel as she crafted her Gentile Gospel. She not only edited these passages from Matthew, but she also moved them in her narrative sequence. She was intent on adapting this borrowed material from its Jewish-Egyptian context to a thought world more familiar to her Antiochian audience. She did the same with the material she used from Mark in the process of baking the fourth layer of the four-tiered wedding cake.

Chapter 8
Unique Content of the Gospel Dedicated to Luke

None of the following verses is found in the Gospel dedicated to Mark or the Gospel dedicated to Matthew. The scribe of the Church of Antioch outdid herself creatively in writing some of the most inspiring passages in the New Testament in exquisite Greek. She created the "Prodigal Son" and the "Good Samaritan," for example. She reflected the concept of Jesus as the human social prophet and religious reformer who was resurrected divine and ascended to heaven. She showed the Kingdom of God as a present entity as well as a future hope. She stressed the imperative of the compassionate use of one's resources. She demonstrated care for all of society's oppressed and championed the equality of women and men. In all of this, she accurately reflected the faith of the community she represented, the Church of Antioch, and Paul's home church.

Introduction
(Luke 1:1-4)

> Since many have undertaken to write an orderly account of the events that have been fulfilled among us, just as they were handed on to us by those who from the beginning were eyewitnesses and servants of the word, I too decided, after investigating everything carefully from the very first, to write an orderly account for you, most excellent Theophilus, so that you may know the truth concerning the things about which you have been instructed.

The first verse makes clear that the scribe knew that there were other gospels in existence, since she had at least two of them, Mark and Matthew, in her possession. Some scholars have speculated that "Theophilus" (which means in Greek "Friend of God") was a new Christian in whose large home this scribe and the Christians in Antioch had begun to meet. One leading theory is that Theophilus was a Roman centurion stationed in Antioch who befriended the Christian community there.

First Part Of Birth Story Of John The Baptist:

A Message From God To Zechariah
(Luke 1:5-25)

> In the days of Herod ("the Great"), King of Judea, there was a priest named Zechariah, who belonged to the priestly group of Abijah. His wife was a descendant of Aaron, and her name was Elizabeth. Both of them were scrupulous in the sight of God, obediently following all the commandments and ordinances of YHWH. They had no children, because Elizabeth was infertile, and both were getting up in years.

> While he was serving as priest before God and his priestly group was on Temple duty, he was chosen by lot, according to the custom of the priesthood, to enter the sanctuary of YHWH and burn incense. When the time came for the incense offering, a huge crowd of people was praying outside. There appeared to him a messenger of YHWH standing on the right side of the altar of incense. When he saw him, Zechariah was shaken and overcome with fear. But the messenger said to him, "Don't be afraid, Zechariah, for your prayer has been heard, and your wife Elizabeth will bear you a son, and you are to name him John.

> "You will be joyful and elated, and many will rejoice at his birth, because he will be great in the sight of YHWH. He will drink no wine or beer, and from the very day of his birth he will be filled with the sacred breath of life. He will cause many of the people of Israel to turn to YHWH their God. He will precede him with the breath of life and power of Elijah. He will turn the hearts of parents back toward their children, and the disobedient back toward the ways of righteousness, and he will make people ready for their Lord."

> Zechariah said to the messenger, "How can I know that this will happen? For I am an old man, and my wife is getting up in years."

> The messenger replied, "I am Gabriel, the one who stands in the presence of God, and I have been sent to speak to you, and to bring you this good news. Listen to me! Because you did not believe my

words, which will come true at the right time, you will become silent and speechless until the day these things happen."

Meanwhile the people were waiting for Zechariah, wondering at his delay in the sanctuary. When he did come out and was unable to speak to them, they realized that he had seen a vision in the sanctuary. He kept making signs to them since he remained unable to speak. When the time of his official duty was ended, he went to his home.

Soon, his wife Elizabeth conceived, and for five months she remained in seclusion. She said, "This is how YHWH has seen fit to deal with me in his good time in taking away the public disgrace (of my infertility)."

The scribe trashed the birth story in the Alexandrian Gospel completely. She chose not to include the three Zoroastrian mobeds (wise men or astrologers) following the star to Bethlehem, presenting their gifts and returning home another way. She would have none of the "slaughter of the innocents," Herod's troops killing all the male children in Bethlehem, two-years-old and younger. She omitted Joseph taking Mary and Jesus to Egypt and returning home after Herod was dead. Instead, she wrote two birth stories, featuring Elizabeth and Mary. In the birth story of John the Baptist, Zechariah is mute most of the time, so Elizabeth can do the talking.

A Message From God To Mary
(Luke 1:26-38)

In the sixth month the messenger Gabriel was sent from God to a young woman engaged to a man whose name was Joseph, of the house of David. The young woman's name was Mary. He entered (the dwelling) and said, "Greetings, favored one, YHWH is with you!" She was greatly troubled by these words, and wondered what this greeting might mean.

The messenger said to her, "Don't be afraid, Mary, for you have found favor with God. Listen to me: you will conceive in your womb and give birth to a son, and you shall name him Jesus. He will be great, and will be called Son of the Most High. YHWH (your) God will give him the throne of his father David, and he will reign over the house of Jacob forever, and his kingdom will have no end."

Mary said to the messenger, "How can this be since I am not involved with a man?"

The messenger said to her, "The sacred breath of life will come over you, and the power of the Most High will cast its shadow on you. Therefore the child to be born will be sacred, and will be called the 'Son of God.' Your relative Elizabeth has also conceived a son in her old age. This is the sixth month of pregnancy for her who was said to be infertile. Nothing is impossible with God."

Mary said, "Here I am, the handmaid of YHWH. May everything you have said come true." And the messenger left her.

The scribe has the messenger (angel) appear to Mary. In Matthew, the messenger appears to Joseph.

Second Part Of Birth Story Of John The Baptist: Meeting Of The Two Pregnant Women
(Luke 1:39-45)

Then Mary set out and went quickly to a Judean town in the hill country, where she entered the house of Zechariah and greeted Elizabeth. When Elizabeth heard Mary's greeting, the fetus jumped in her womb. And Elizabeth was filled with the sacred breath of life and proclaimed at the top of her voice:

Blessed are you among women,
and blessed is the fruit of your womb!
And who am I, that the mother of my Lord should visit me?
For as soon as I heard your words of greeting,
the fetus in my womb jumped for joy.
Blessed is she who believed that what YHWH
promised her would come true.

The scribe creates the one and only conversation between two women in the New Testament. The word "womb(s)" occurs only nine (9) times in the New Testament and seven (7) of those are in Luke (one in John and one in Romans).

Mary's Song Known As "Magnificat"
(Luke 1:46-55)

And Mary said,

My soul magnifies YHWH,
and my life breath rejoices in God my Savior,

for he has looked with favor on the lowly status of his handmaid.
Surely, from now on every generation will call me blessed.
The Mighty One has done great things for me,
and sacred is his name.
His mercy will come to generation
after generation of those who worship him.
He has shown the strength of his arm.
He has put the arrogant to rout, along with their private schemes.
He has pulled the mighty down from their thrones,
and lifted up the lowly.
He has filled the hungry with good things,
and sent the rich away empty.
He has helped his servant Israel, remembering his mercy,
according to the promise he made to our ancestors,
to Abraham and to his descendants forever.

The poetess scribe adapts a poem spoken by Hannah in I Samuel 2 by removing some of the violent phrases and produces a kinder, gentler version.

Birth Of John The Baptist
(Luke 1:56-66)

And Mary stayed with Elizabeth about three months, and then returned to her home. The time came for Elizabeth to give birth, and she had a son. Her neighbors and relatives heard that YHWH had shown her great mercy, and they rejoiced with her. On the eighth day they came to circumcise the child; and they were going to name him Zechariah after his father.

But his mother said, "No! He shall be called John."

They said to her, "No one in your family has that name."

They made signs to his father, asking what he wanted to have him called. He asked for a writing tablet, and they were amazed when he wrote, "His name is John." Immediately his mouth was opened and his tongue loosed, and he spoke, blessing God. All their neighbors were awe-struck. All these things were talked about through all the hill country of Judea. All who heard about them took them to heart and wondered, "What is this child going to be?" For the hand of YHWH was with him.

The wife, Elizabeth, is in charge here.

Zechariah's Song Known As "Benedictus"
(Luke 1:67-80)

Then his father Zechariah was filled with the sacred breath of life and prophesied:

Blessed be YHWH, the God of Israel,
for he has visited his people and ransomed them.
He has raised up a horn of salvation
for us in the house of his servant David.
This is what he promised in the words of his sacred prophets of old:
deliverance from our enemies and from
the hands of all who hate us;
mercy to our ancestors,
and remembrance of his sacred covenant.
This is the oath he swore to our ancestor Abraham:
to grant that we be rescued from the hands of our enemies,
to serve him without fear, in holiness and righteousness
before him all our days.
And you, child, will be called a prophet of the Most High.
For you will go before the Lord to prepare his way,
to give his people knowledge of salvation
through the forgiveness of their sins.
In the heartfelt mercy of our God, the dawn from on high will visit us,
to shine on those who sit in darkness, in the shadow of death,
to guide our feet to the way of peace.
The child grew and became strong in the breath of life, and he
was in the wilderness until the day he appeared publicly to Israel.

This is an original poem composed by the poetess, using allusions to several Psalms.

Birth Of Jesus
(Luke 2:1-7)

In those days a decree was issued by Emperor Augustus that all people of the (Roman) world should be counted. This first census occurred when Quirinius was governor of Syria. All the people had to travel to their ancestral cities. Joseph also went up to the city of David, called Bethlehem, because he was a descendant of David, to be counted in the census with Mary, to whom he was engaged and who was pregnant. While they were there, the time came for her to give birth. She gave birth to her first-born son and wrapped him in strips of cloth, and laid him in a feeding trough, because there was no place for them in the (sleeping area of the) dwelling. Joseph named him Jesus.

There is no collaborating record of such a census at this time, but she used it as a vehicle to get Joseph and Mary to Bethlehem. Since Joseph was said to be a member of the tribe of Judah, he and Mary would have been sleeping in the cave home of one of his many relatives. Poverty and easily dug caves in limestone hills made cave homes necessary. The scribe wrote that "there was no place for them in the inn," not knowing that there were no "inns" in Bethlehem. In Luke, Jesus is born as a human being, not a god.

Messengers' Song Known As "Gloria" And Shepherds' Visit
(Luke 2:8-20)

> In that area there were shepherds living outdoors, watching over their sheep at night. A messenger of YHWH stood near them, and the glory of YHWH shone around them. They were fearful. The messenger said to them,
>
> > Don't be afraid. Listen: I bring you good news of a great joy
> > which is to benefit the whole nation.
> > Today in the city of David, a Savior was born to you.
> > He is the Messiah, the Lord.
> > And this will be a sign for you: you will find a baby
> > wrapped in strips of cloth and lying in a feeding trough.
>
> And suddenly there appeared with the messenger a whole troop of the army of the heavens praising God:
>
> > Glory to God in the highest heavens,
> > and on earth peace among those he favors!
>
> When the messengers went away and returned to the heavens, the shepherds said to one another, "Let's go over to Bethlehem and see what has happened, this event YHWH has told us about." They hurried along, and found Mary and Joseph, and the baby lying in a feeding trough. When they saw it they reported what had been told them concerning this child, and all who heard it were amazed at what the shepherds told them. But Mary took all this in and reflected on it. The shepherds returned, glorifying and praising God for all they had heard and seen. Everything turned out just as they had been told.

The pastoral scene with the shepherds and angels is much more tender than the action in Matthew. We should understand these shepherds to be Joseph's cousins.

Joseph And Mary Present Jesus In The Temple
(Luke 2:21-27)

> Eight days later, when the time came to circumcise him, they gave him the name Jesus, the name given by the messenger before he was conceived in the womb. When the time came for their purification according to the Teaching of Moses, they brought him up to Jerusalem to present him to YHWH (as it is written in the Teaching of YHWH, "Every male that opens the womb shall be called sacred to YHWH") and to offer a sacrifice according to what is said in the Teaching of YHWH, "a pair of turtle-doves, or two young pigeons."
>
> Now there was a man in Jerusalem, named Simeon, a decent and devout man, who was waiting for the consolation of Israel, and the sacred breath of life was with him. It had been revealed to him by the sacred breath of life that he would not see death before he had seen the Messiah of YHWH. And so, inspired by the breath of life, he came to the Temple area.

In Matthew, Joseph and Mary didn't want anything to do with Jerusalem, because Herod was in Jerusalem and wanted to kill Jesus. This scribe marches the little family right into the Temple area in Jerusalem with no fear.

Simeon's Song Known As "Nunc Dimittis"
(Luke 2:28-35)

> And when the parents brought in the child Jesus, to perform for him what was customary according to the Teaching, he took him in his arms and blessed God and said:
>
> > Master, now you can dismiss your servant in peace,
> > according to your word.
> > For my eyes have seen your salvation
> > which you have prepared in the sight of all the peoples,
> > a revelatory light for foreigners and glory for your people Israel.
>
> His father and mother were astonished at what was being said about him. And Simeon blessed them and said to Mary his mother, "Listen to me: this child is linked to the fall and rise of many in Israel, and is destined to be a sign that is rejected. You too will have your heart broken, and the schemes of many minds will be exposed."

Notice the original poem, and notice that Simeon speaks to Mary, not Joseph.

Anna, The Prophetess, Offers Thanksgiving For The Child
(Luke 2:36-38)

> There was a prophetess, Anna, the daughter of Phanuel, of the tribe of Asher. She was very old, since she had been married as a young woman and lived with her husband seven years, and then alone as a widow till she was eighty-four. She never left the Temple area, and she worshiped night and day with fasting and prayer. Coming on the scene at that very moment she gave thanks to God, and began to speak about the child to all who were waiting for the liberation of Jerusalem.

Anna is the only woman prophet mentioned in the New Testament.

Return To Nazareth
(Luke 2:39-40)

> When they had finished everything required by the Teaching of YHWH, they returned to Galilee, to their own town of Nazareth. The child grew and became strong, filled with wisdom, and the favor of God was upon him.

Another reference to the humanity of Jesus at this point in his life.

Jesus' Bar Mitzvah: Passover When Jesus Was Twelve
(Luke 2:41-52)

> Now his parents regularly went to Jerusalem every year for the feast of the Passover. When he was twelve years old, they went up for the feast as usual. When the feast was over and they were returning home, young Jesus stayed behind in Jerusalem without his parents knowing about it. Assuming that he was in the traveling party, they went a day's journey, and then they began to look for him among their relatives and acquaintances. When they didn't find him, they returned to Jerusalem to search for him.

> After three days they found him in the Temple area, sitting among the teachers, listening to them and asking them questions. Everyone who heard him was amazed at his understanding and his responses. When his parents saw him they were overwhelmed. His mother said to him, "Child, why have you done this to us? Your father and I have been worried sick looking for you."

> He said to them, "Why were you looking for me? Didn't you know that I have to be in my Father's house?"

They did not understand what he was talking about. He went down with them and returned to Nazareth, and was obedient to them. His mother took careful note of all these things. And Jesus, precocious as he was, continued to excel in learning and to gain respect in the eyes of God and others.

Notice that Mary does the talking here and is the parent taking careful notes.

John's Teaching At Jesus' Baptism
(Luke 3:10-14)

And the crowds asked him, "So what should we do?"

John answered them, "Whoever has two shirts should share with someone who has none. Whoever has food should do the same." Toll collectors also came to be baptized, and asked him, "Teacher, what should we do?" He said to them, "Charge nothing above the official rates." Soldiers also asked him, "And what about us?" He said to them, "No more shakedowns! No more frame-ups either! And be content with your pay."

The issue here is the compassionate use of money and other goods.

Gentile Version Of Jesus' Family Tree
(Luke 3:24-38)

He was supposedly the son of Joseph, son of Eli, son of Matthat, son of Levi, son of Melchi, son of Jannai, son of Joseph, son of Mattathias, son of Amos, son of Nahum, son of Hesli, son of Naggai, son of Maath, son of Mattathias, son of Semein, son of Josech, son of Joda, son of Johanan, son of Rhesa, son of Zerubbabel, son of Salathiel, son of Neri, son of Melchi, son of Addi, son of Cosam, son of Elmadam, son of Er, son of Joshua, son of Eliezer, son of Jorim, son of Matthat, son of Levi, son of Simeon, son of Judah, son of Joseph, son of Jonam, son of Eliakim, son of Melea, son of Menna, son of Mattatha, son of Nathan, son of David, son of Jesse, son of Obed, son of Boaz, son of Sala, son of Nahshon, son of Amminadab, son of Admin, son of Arni, son of Hezron, son of Perez, son of Judah, son of Jacob, son of Isaac, son of Abraham, son of Terah, son of Nahor, son of Serug, son of Reu, son of Peleg, son of Eber, son of Shelah, son of Cainan, son of Arphachshad, son of Shem, son of Noah, son of Lamech, son of Methuselah, son of Enoch, son of Jared, son of Mahalalel, son of Kenan, son of Enosh, son of Seth, son of Adam, son of God.

The Gentile genealogy goes all the way back to Adam, not stopping with Abraham as the Jewish version does in Matthew. Also, notice that Adam is called a "son of God," just as Jesus is called a "son of God."

Jesus Calls His Best Friends To Be His First Disciples
(Luke 5:1-11)

Blessings And Curses
(Luke 6:20-26)

> Then he looked up at his disciples and said,
>
> "Blessed are you who are poor; the Kingdom of God belongs to you.
> Blessed are you who are hungry right now; you will be filled up later.
> Blessed are you who are crying right now; you will be laughing later."
> "Blessed are you when people hate you, shun you,
> curse you and smear your reputation because you believe
> in the Son of Man. Be happy when they do that because
> I guarantee your reward will be great in heaven.
> Their ancestors did the same things to the prophets."
> "But damn you who are rich; you already have your good stuff.
> Damn you whose bellies are full now; you will be hungry later.
> Damn you who are all giggly now; you will mourn and cry later.
> Damn you that everybody tries to butter up;
> That's what their ancestors did to the phony prophets."

The scribe adds the curses to Matthew's beatitudes as condemnation of the wealthy citizens of Antioch who are not exercising the compassionate use of money and resources.

Jesus Resurrects A Widow's Son At Nain
(Luke 7:11-17)

> Soon afterward he came to a town of Nain, and his disciples and a great crowd went with him. As he neared the gate of the city, a dead man was being carried out, the only son of his mother, and she was a widow. A large crowd from the city was with her.
>
> When the Lord saw her, his heart went out to her and he said to her, "Don't cry." He went up and touched the bier, and the bearers stood still. And he said, "Young man, I say to you, get up!" The dead man sat up, and began to speak. And (Jesus) gave him back to his mother. They were all awestruck, and they glorified God, saying, "A

great prophet has been raised up among us!" and "God has visited his people!" This story about him spread throughout Judea and all the surrounding area.

Remember, this story is only written in Luke. When the widow's son dies, the widow is penniless and destitute. Jesus gives her back her son and her life.

Jesus Has Dinner With A Pharisee
And Is Anointed By A Woman
(Luke 7:36-50)

He entered the Pharisee's house and reclined at the table. A local woman, who was a sinner, found out that he was having dinner at the Pharisee's house. She suddenly showed up with an alabaster jar of myrrh, and stood there behind him weeping at his feet. Her tears wet his feet, and she wiped them dry with her hair. She kissed his feet, and anointed them with the myrrh.

The Pharisee who had invited him saw this and said to himself, "If this man were a prophet, he would know who this is and what kind of woman is touching him, since she is a sinner."

Jesus answered him, "Simon, I have something to tell you."

He responded, "What is it, Teacher?"

"This moneylender had two debtors. One owed five hundred silver coins, and the other fifty. Since neither one of them could pay, he wrote off both debts. Now which of them will love him more?"

Simon answered, "I would imagine the one for whom he wrote off the larger debt."

He said to him "You are right." Then turning to the woman, he said to Simon, "Do you see this woman? I walked into your house, and you didn't offer me water for my feet, but she has washed my feet with her tears and dried them with her hair. You didn't offer me a kiss, but she has not stopped kissing my feet since I arrived. You didn't anoint my head with oil, but she has anointed my feet with myrrh. Therefore I tell you, her sins, many as they are, have been forgiven, as this outpouring of her love shows. But the one who is forgiven little shows little love."

He said to her, "Your sins have been forgiven."

Then those having dinner with him, began to mutter to themselves, "Who is this who even forgives sins?"

And he said to the woman, "Your faith has saved you. Go in peace."

This story is unique and different from the anointing of Jesus' head in Mark and Matthew. This woman anoints Jesus' feet with her tears and dries his feet with her hair. The story of anointing in Mark and Matthew happens in the home of Simon, the leper, not in the home of a Pharisee. We don't know if Simon is Simon Peter or Simon the host, the Pharisee.

Women With The Disciples
(Luke 8:1-3)

> Soon afterward, he pressed on through towns and villages (of Galilee), preaching and announcing the good news of the Kingdom of God. The "twelve" were with him, and also some women whom he had cured of evil spirits and diseases: Mary, the one from Magdala, from whom seven demons had taken their leave; and Joanna, the wife of Chuza, Herod's steward; and Susanna, and many others, who provided for them out of their resources.

Three women are named, and it is said that there were many other women who supported Jesus' ministry.

An Incident With Samaritan Villagers
(Luke 9:52-56)

> (As he traveled south, Jesus) sent messengers on ahead of him. They entered a Samaritan village, to get things ready for him. But the Samaritans would not welcome him, because he had made up his mind to go on to Jerusalem. When his disciples James and John realized this, they said, "Lord, do you want us to call down fire from the heavens and annihilate them?" But he turned and reprimanded them. Then they continued on to the next village.

The Church of Antioch needs Jesus to treat the oppressed with respect and equality.

Jesus Deals With Question On Inheriting Eternal Life
(Luke 10:25-28)

> On one occasion, a legal expert stood up to put him to the test with a question: "Teacher, what do I have to do to inherit eternal life?"

He said to him, "How do you read what is written in the Teaching?"

And he answered, "You are to love YHWH your God with all your heart, with all your soul, with all your energy, and with all your mind; and your neighbor as yourself."

Jesus said to him, "You have given the correct answer. Do this and you will have life."

Nothing is said here about the need for baptism or repentance or being anointed by Holy Spirit. Eternal life is provided for those who love God and neighbor with unconditional love.

Parable Of A Good Samaritan
(Luke 10:29-37)

But trying to nit-pick, he asked Jesus, "And who is my neighbor?"

Jesus replied, "There was a man going down from Jerusalem to Jericho, and he fell into the hands of robbers, who stripped him, beat him up, and went off, leaving him half dead. Now by coincidence a priest was going down that road. When he caught sight of him, he went out of his way to avoid him. In the same way, when a Levite came to the place, he took one look at him and crossed the road to avoid him.

"But this Samaritan who was traveling that way came to where he was, and was moved to pity at the sight of him. He went up to him and bandaged his wounds, pouring olive oil and wine on them. He hoisted him on his own animal and brought him to a hospitality house, and looked after him. The next day he took out two silver coins, which he gave to the host, and said, 'Look after him, and on my way back I'll reimburse you for any extra expense you have had.'

"Which of these three, do you think, was a neighbor to the man who fell into the hands of the robbers?"

He said, "The one who showed him mercy."

Jesus said to him, "Go and do the same."

She is the only scribe to include this parable, and she does so for two reasons: first, the Samaritan is a Gentile (and that distinction is significant) and ostracized and oppressed, and Antioch believes that Jesus and the Gospel is for all humankind; secondly, it's about the compassionate use of money, which is very important to the Christians in Antioch.

Jesus Visits With Mary And Martha In Bethany
(Luke 10:38-42)

> As they continued on their journey, he came to the village (of Bethany), where a woman named Martha welcomed him into her home. She had a sister named Mary, who sat at the Lord's feet and listened to his words. But Martha was distracted because she was doing all the serving. So she went up to (Jesus) and said, "Lord, doesn't it matter to you that my sister has left me with all the serving? Tell her to give me a hand."

> But the Lord answered her, "Martha, Martha, you are worried and upset about a lot of things. But only one thing is necessary. Mary has made the better choice and it is something she will never lose."

If the Gospel dedicated to John is correct and Mary and Martha live in Bethany, then this scribe doesn't have a clue about the geography of Judea and Galilee. At this point in the process, Jesus is nowhere near Jerusalem, and Bethany is a suburb of Jerusalem. But the main point is that she introduces us to these two women for the first time.

Deeper Spirituality And Middle Eastern Hospitality
(Luke 11:5-8)

True Blessedness
(Luke 11:27-28)

> A woman in the crowd spoke up and said to him, "Blessed is the womb that bore you and the breasts that nursed you!"

> But he said, "Blessed rather are those who hear the word of God and obey it!"

A woman blesses Jesus, the first woman to do so since Anna, the prophetess. The word "breasts" occurs four (4) times in the New Testament, all in Luke.

Parable Of A Rich Farmer
(Luke 12:13-21)

> Someone in the crowd spoke out to him, "Teacher, tell my brother to divide the inheritance with me."

But he said to him, "Mister, who appointed me your judge or arbiter?" And he said to them, "Watch out! Guard against greed in all its forms. After all, possessions, even in abundance, don't guarantee someone life."

Then he told them (another) parable, saying, "There was a rich man whose fields produced a bumper crop. He thought to himself, 'What do I do now, since I have nowhere to store my crops? I know!' he said, 'I'll tear down my barns, and build larger ones so I can store all my grain and my goods. Then I will say to myself, you have plenty put away for years to come. Take it easy, eat, drink, enjoy yourself.'

"But God said to him, 'You fool! This very night your life will be demanded back from you. All this stuff you have collected, whose will it be now?'

"That's the way it is with those who save up for themselves, but aren't rich where God is concerned."

The point again here is the Antiochian emphasis on the compassionate use of money and resources.

Baptism By Fire
(Luke 12:49-50)

Parable Of A Fig Tree
(Luke 13:6-9)

Jesus Frees A Woman From Affliction On A Sabbath
(Luke 13:10-17)

Jesus was teaching in one of the synagogues on the Sabbath. A woman showed up who for eighteen years had been afflicted by a spirit. She was bent over and unable to straighten up even a little. When Jesus noticed her, he called her over and said, "Woman, you are freed from your affliction." He laid his hands on her, and immediately she stood up straight and began to praise God.

But the leader of the synagogue was indignant because Jesus had cured on the Sabbath. He lectured the crowd, "There are six days which we devote to work. So, come on one of those days and be cured, but not on the Sabbath."

Then the Lord answered him, "You phonies! Every last one of you unties your ox or your donkey from the feeding trough on the Sabbath, and leads it away to water, don't you? This woman, a daughter of Abraham whom the Tempter has kept in bondage for eighteen long years, should she not be released from these bonds just because it is the Sabbath?" As he said this, all his adversaries were put to shame. But most folks rejoiced at all the wonderful things he was doing.

In the Gospel dedicated to Matthew, the person being healed is a man with a withered hand. She changes it to a woman with osteoporosis.

Some Pharisees Warn Jesus About Herod
(Luke 13:31-33)

Jesus Cures A Man With Severe Skin Swellings On A Sabbath
(Luke 14:1-6)

Parable On Humility
(Luke 14:7-14)

> (Then) he told a parable for those who had been invited, when he noticed how they chose the places of honor.
>
> He said to them, "When someone invites you to a wedding banquet, don't take the place of honor, in case someone more important than you has been invited. Then the one who invited you both will come and say to you, 'Make room for this person,' and then you will be embarrassed to have to take the lowest place. Instead, when you are invited, go take the lowest place, so when your host comes he will say to you, 'Friend, come up higher.' Then you will be honored in front of all those reclining around the table with you. Those who promote themselves will be demoted, and those who demote themselves will be promoted."
>
> Jesus said also to his host, "When you give a lunch or a dinner, don't invite your friends, or your brothers and sisters, or relatives or rich neighbors. They might invite you in return, and so you would be repaid. Instead, when you throw a dinner party, invite the poor, the crippled, the lame, and the blind. In that case, you will be blessed, because they cannot repay you. You will be repaid at the resurrection of the just."

In Antioch, Jesus is an advocate for social justice and religious reform.

About Discipleship
(Luke 14:25-33)

Parable Of A Woman And One Lost Coin
(Luke 15:8-10)

> "Or again, is there any woman with ten silver coins (each worth an average day's wage), who if she loses one, wouldn't light a lamp and sweep the house and search carefully until she finds it? When she finds it, she invites her friends and neighbors over and says, 'Celebrate with me, because I have found the silver coin I had lost.'

> "I'm telling you, it is just like this among God's messengers. They celebrate when one sinner has a change of heart."

Another unparalleled story about a woman!

The Prodigal Son
(Luke 15:1-2,11-32)

> Now the toll collectors and sinners kept crowding around Jesus so they could hear him. But the Pharisees and the scholars complained to each other, "This fellow welcomes sinners and (even) eats with them." So he told (both groups) this parable:

> "Once there was this man who had two sons. The younger of them said to his father, 'Father, give me (now) the share of the property that's coming to me (when you die).' (Incredibly, the father) divided his resources between them.

> "Not too many days later, the younger son got all his things together and left (his) home (village) for a faraway country, where he squandered his property by living extravagantly. Just when he had spent it all, a severe famine swept through that country, and he began to do without. So he went and hired himself out to one of the citizens of that country, who sent him out on his farm to feed the pigs. He longed to satisfy his hunger with the carob pods, which the pigs usually ate, but no one offered him any.

"Coming to his senses he said, 'Lots of my father's hired hands have more than enough to eat, while here I am dying of starvation! I will get up and go to my father, and I'll say to him, "Father, I have sinned against the heavens and affronted you. I don't deserve to be called a son of yours any longer. Treat me like one of your hired hands."' And he got up and returned to his father('s village).

"But while he was still (outside the village gate), his father caught sight of him and was moved to compassion. He ran out (through the gate) to him, threw his arms around his neck and kissed him. And the son said to him, 'Father, I have sinned against the heavens and affronted you. I don't deserve to be called a son of yours any longer.'

"But the father said to his slaves, 'Quick! Bring out (my) finest robe, and put it on him. Put (one of my) ring(s) on his finger, and (my) sandals on his feet. Fetch the fat calf and slaughter it. Let's have a feast and celebrate, because this son of mine was dead and has come back to life. He was lost and now is found.' And they started celebrating.

"His elder son was out in the field, and as he got closer to the house, he heard music and dancing. He called one of the servant-boys over and asked what was going on. The servant-boy said to him, 'Your brother has come home, and your father has slaughtered the fat calf, because he has him back safe and sound.'

"The elder son became angry and refused to go in (the house). So, his father came out and began to plead with him. But he answered his father, 'See here, all these many years I have slaved for you. I never once disobeyed any of your orders. Yet you never once provided me with a kid goat so I could celebrate with my friends. But when this son of yours shows up, the one who has squandered your estate with prostitutes, for him you slaughter the fat calf!'

"But the father said to him, 'My child, you are always at my side. Everything that is mine is yours. But we just had to celebrate and rejoice, because this brother of yours was dead, and has come back to life. He was lost and now is found.'"

This is a long, beautiful story she creates. The father is Jesus, the younger son represents the Gentiles, and the older son represents the Jews. The point is that Jesus loves and cares for both Jew and Gentile, and the Gospel is for all the world.

Parable Of A Shrewd Manager
(Luke 16:1-8)

111

Lesson On The Parable Of A Shrewd Manager
(Luke 16:8-15)

Parable Of A Rich Man And A Poor Man
(Luke 16:19-31)

(He told them another parable:)

"There was a rich man, who wore clothing fit for a king and who dined lavishly every day. A poor man, named Lazarus, covered with sores, languished at his gate. He longed to eat what fell from the rich man's table. Dogs would come and lick his sores. The poor man died and was carried by the messengers of the heavens to be with Abraham. The rich man died too, and was buried.

"From (the Valley of Hinnom), where he was being tortured, he looked up and saw Abraham a long way off and Lazarus with him. He called out, 'Father Abraham, have pity on me! Send Lazarus to dip the tip of his finger in water and cool my tongue, for I am in torment in these flames.'

"But Abraham said, 'My child, remember that you had good fortune in your lifetime, while Lazarus had it bad. Now he is being comforted here, and you are in torment. And besides all this, a great chasm has been set between us and you, so that even those who want to cross over from here to you cannot, and no one can cross over from that side to ours.'

"But he said, 'Father, then I beg you, send him to my father's house, since I have five brothers, so he can warn them not to wind up in this place of torture.'

"But Abraham said, 'They have Moses and the prophets. Why don't they listen to them?'

"And he said, 'But they won't do that, Father Abraham. However, if someone appears to them from the dead, they will have a change of heart.'

"(Abraham) said to him, 'If they won't listen to Moses and the prophets, they won't be convinced even if someone were to be raised from the dead.'

Another long, beautiful, original story she tells. The message is that one must exercise compassionate use of money, or else.

On Slave Wages
(Luke 17:7-10)

Jesus Cures Ten Lepers, Including A Samaritan
(Luke 17:11-19)

> On the way to Jerusalem he passed (through the boundary) between Samaria and Galilee. As he entered this village, he was met by ten lepers, who kept their distance. They shouted, "Jesus, Master, have mercy on us!"
>
> When he saw them, he said to them, "Go show yourselves to the priests." And as they departed they were (cured and) made clean.
>
> Then one of them, realizing that he had been cured, came back. He praised God out loud, prostrated himself at Jesus' feet, and thanked him. He was a Samaritan.
>
> Jesus said, "Ten were cured, weren't they? What became of the other nine? Didn't any of them return to praise God besides this outcast?"
>
> He said to him, "Get up and be on your way. Your faith has cured you."

Another story in which the good person is the Samaritan, the despised leper

Jesus Answers Question About The Coming Of The Kingdom
(Luke 17:20-21)

> When asked by the Pharisees when the Kingdom of God would come, he answered them, "You won't be able to observe the coming of the Kingdom of God. People are not going to be able to say, 'Look, here it is!' or 'Over there!' On the contrary, the Kingdom of God is right here in your presence."

In Mark, it was called the "Empire of God," and it will be inaugurated tomorrow in Rome and on all the Earth. In Matthew, it was called the "Kingdom of Heaven," and it will begin for the individual when one dies, or for the human race at the end of time, whichever comes first, and the Kingdom of Heaven is up yonder, out there among the stars. In Luke, it is called the "Kingdom of God," and it has already begun on Earth and will continue on Earth and in Heaven.

Parable Of A Judge And A Persistent Widow
(Luke 18:1-8)

Jesus told them a parable about the need to pray at all times and never to lose heart. He said, "Once there was a judge in a certain town who neither feared God nor cared about people. In that same town was a widow who kept coming to him and demanding, 'Give me a ruling against the person I'm suing.'

"For a while he refused, but eventually he said to himself, 'I'm not afraid of God and I don't care about people, but this widow keeps pestering me. So I'm going to give her a favorable ruling, or else she'll keep coming back until she wears me down.'"

And the Lord said, "Don't you hear what that corrupt judge says? Do you really think God will not hand out justice to his chosen ones, those who call on him day and night? Do you really think he will put them off? I'm telling you, he will give them justice and give it quickly. Still, when the Son of Adam comes, will he find faith on the earth?"

Another story about a widow that is original with this woman scribe

Parable Of A Pharisee And A Toll Collector
(Luke 18:9-14)

Jesus Meets Zacchaeus
(Luke 19:1-10)

Then he entered Jericho and was making his way through it. There was a man named Zacchaeus who lived there. He was the head toll collector and a rich man. He was trying to see who Jesus was, but couldn't, because of the crowd, since he was short. So he ran on ahead to a point Jesus was to pass and climbed a sycamore tree to get a view of him.

When Jesus reached that spot, he looked up and said, "Zacchaeus, hurry up and climb down. After all, I have to stay at your house today." So he scurried down and welcomed him warmly.

Everyone who saw this complained, "He is going to spend the day with some sinner." Zacchaeus stood his ground and said to the Lord, "Look, sir, I'll give half of what I own to the poor, and if I have extorted anything from anyone, I'll pay back four times as much."

Jesus said to him, "Today salvation has come to this house. This man is a real son of Abraham. Remember, the Son of Adam came to seek out and to save what was lost."

The Church of Antioch is insistent that the compassionate use of money is essential to Christian faith.

Parable Of Money In Trust
(Luke 19:11-27)

While they were still paying attention to this exchange, Jesus proceeded to tell a parable, because he was near Jerusalem and people thought that the Kingdom of God would appear immediately.

He said, "A nobleman went off to a distant land intending to acquire a kingship for himself and then return. He called ten of his slaves, and gave them each one hundred silver coins, and told them: 'Do business with this while I'm away.'

"His fellow citizens, however, hated him and sent a delegation right on his heels, with the petition: 'We don't want this man to rule us.' As it turned out, he got the kingship and returned. He had those slaves summoned to whom he had given the money, in order to find out what profit they had made.

"The first came in and reported, 'Master, you investment has increased ten times over.' He said to him, 'Well done, you excellent slave! Because you have been trustworthy in this small matter, you are to be in charge of ten cities.'

"The second came in and reported, 'Master, your investment has increased five times over.' And he said to him, 'And you are to be in charge of five cities.'

"Then the last came in and said, 'Master, here is your money. I kept it tucked away safe in a handkerchief. You see, I was afraid of you, because you are a demanding man. You withdraw what you didn't deposit, and reap what you didn't sow.'

"He said to him, 'You incompetent slave! Your own words convict you. So you knew that I was demanding, did you? That I reap what I didn't sow and withdraw what I didn't deposit? So why didn't you put my money in the bank? Then I could have collected it with interest when I got back.'

"Then he said to his attendants, 'Take the money away from this fellow and give it to the one who has ten times as much.' 'But my lord,' they said to him, 'he already has ten times as much.'

> "He replied, 'I tell you, to everyone who has, more will be given. And from those who don't have, even what they do have will be taken away. But now, about those enemies of mine, the ones who didn't want me to rule them. Bring them here and execute them in my presence.'"

The only good reason for acquiring money is in order to give it away for compassionate purposes. Antioch considers all money to be held in trust.

Teachings Of Jesus In Jerusalem
(Luke 21:37-38)

On Having Enough
(Luke 22:35-38)

Reattaching The Slave's Ear
(Luke 22:49-51)

> And when those (disciples) who were around him realized what was coming next, they said, "Master, now do we use our swords?" At that moment, one of them struck the slave of the High Priest, and cut off his right ear. But Jesus said, "Stop! That will do! And he touched the slave's ear and restored him.

She doesn't believe that Jesus would leave the slave's ear lying on the ground. Mark and Matthew both say that one of the disciples cuts off the slave's ear, but she specifies that it is the slave's "right" ear, raising all kinds of problems.

Jesus' Civil Trial
(Luke 23:1-16)

> Then the whole Sanhedrin got up and took Jesus to Pilate.
>
> They introduced their accusations by saying, "We have found this man to be a corrupting influence on our people, opposing the payment of taxes to the Roman emperor and claiming that he himself is Messiah and king."

Pilate questioned him, "Are you the 'King of the Judeans'?"

Jesus answered him, "If you say so."

Pilate said to the ranking priests and the crowds, "In my judgment there is no case against this man."

But they persisted, saying, "He foments unrest among the people by going around teaching everywhere in Judea, and as far away as Galilee and everywhere in between."

When Pilate heard this, he asked whether the man were a Galilean. Once he confirmed that he was from Herod's jurisdiction, he sent him to Herod (Antipas), who happened to be in Jerusalem at the time.

Now Herod was delighted to see Jesus. In fact, he had been eager to see him for quite some time, since he had heard so much about him, and was hoping to see him perform some sign. So he questioned him at some length, but (Jesus) would not answer him at all.

All this time the ranking priests and the scholars were standing around, hurling accusation after accusation against him. Herod and his soldiers treated him with contempt and made fun of him. They put a magnificent robe around him and then sent him back to Pilate. And Herod and Pilate became fast friends that very day, even though beforehand they had been constantly at odds.

Pilate then called together the ranking priests, the rulers and the people, and addressed them: "You brought me this man as one who has been corrupting the people. Now look, after interrogating him in your presence, I have found in this man no grounds at all for your charges against him. Nor has Herod, since he sent him back to us. Indeed, he has done nothing to deserve death. So I will teach him a lesson and set him free."

She absolves Pilate of responsibility and blames the Jews for Jesus' execution.

On The Way To Execution
(Luke 23:26-31)

As they were marching him away, they grabbed a bystander named Simon, who had come (to Jerusalem) from the country of Cyrene. He (turned out to be) the father of Alexander and Rufus. They loaded the crosspiece on him, to carry behind Jesus. A huge crowd of people followed him, including women who mourned and lamented him.

117

Jesus turned to them and said, "Daughters of Jerusalem, do not weep for me. Weep instead for yourselves and for your children. Look, the time is coming when they will say, 'Blessed are those who are sterile, and the wombs that never gave birth, and the breasts that never nursed an infant!'"

Then they will beg the mountains: 'Fall on us';
and (they will beg) the hills: 'Cover us.'
If they behave this way when the wood is green,
what will happen when it dries out?

She adds this short speech from the mouth of suffering Jesus to the women bystanders and followers.

Crucified Thief
(Luke 23:39-43)

Even one of the criminals who was crucified with him cursed and taunted him, saying, "Aren't you supposed to be the Messiah? Save yourself and us!"

But the other (criminal) rebuked the first, saying, "Don't you even fear God, since you are under the same sentence? We are getting justice, since we are getting what we deserve. But this man has done nothing improper." And he implored, "Jesus, remember me when you come into your Kingdom."

(Jesus) said to him, "I swear to you, today you will be with me in Paradise."

She contributes another original piece to indicate compassion for the suffering thief who believed that Jesus would reign in the Kingdom of God after he died.

Women At Resurrection
(Luke 24:10-12)

It was Mary of Magdala, Joanna, Mary the mother of James (and Jesus) and the other women who told this to the apostles. But these words seemed to them and idle tale, and they did not believe them. But Peter got up and ran to the tomb. He stooped down and looked in and saw the linen cloths but no body. Then he went back, amazed at what had happened.

The involvement of women is highlighted, even though it is in a negative sense that they were not believed.

Jesus Appears At Emmaus
(Luke 24:13-35)

Now, that same day two (followers) were walking to a village named Emmaus, about seven miles from Jerusalem. They were engaged in conversation about all that had taken place. And it so happened, during the course of their discussion, that Jesus himself approached and began to walk along with them. But they couldn't recognize him.

He said to them, "What were you discussing as you walked along?"

Then they paused, looking depressed. One of them, named Cleopas, said to him in reply, "Are you the only visitor to Jerusalem who does not know what has happened there these last few days?"

He said to them, "What are you talking about?"

They said to him, "About Jesus of Nazareth, who was a prophet powerful in deed and word in the eyes of God and all the people, and about how our ranking priests and rulers turned him in to be sentenced to death, and crucified him. We were hoping that he would be the one who was going to ransom Israel. And as if this weren't enough, it's been three days now since all this happened.

"Meanwhile, some women from our group gave us quite a shock. They were at the tomb early this morning and did not find his body. They came back claiming even to have seen a vision of (a) messenger from the heavens, who said that he was alive. Some of those with us went to the tomb, and found it exactly as the women had described. But nobody saw him."

He said to them, "You people are so slow-witted, so reluctant to believe everything the prophets have said! Wasn't the Messiah destined to undergo these things and enter into his glory?" Then, starting with Moses and all the Prophets, he interpreted for them every passage of Scripture that referred to himself.

They had come close to the village to which they were going, and he acted as if he were going on. But they invited him, saying, "Stay with us, since it is almost evening and the day is practically over." So he went in to stay with them.

And so, as soon as he took his place at table with them, he took a loaf and gave a blessing, and broke it, and started passing it out to them. Then their eyes were opened and they recognized him, but he vanished from their sight.

They said to each other, "Weren't our hearts burning (within us) while he was talking to us on the road, and explaining the Scriptures to us?" They got up at once and returned to Jerusalem, and when they found the eleven and those with them gathered together, they said, "The Lord really has been raised, and has appeared to Simon!" Then they described what had happened on the road, and how they came to recognize him in the breaking of the bread.

The Church of Antioch believed that Jesus was resurrected as a god, able to appear and disappear at will (which he couldn't do before).

Jesus Talks With The Disciples In Jerusalem
(Luke 24:36-45)

While they were talking about this, Jesus himself appeared among them and said to them, "Peace be with you." But they were terrified and frightened, and figured that they were seeing a ghost.

He said to them, "Why are you upset? Why do such thoughts run through your minds? You can see from my hands and my feet that it's really me. Touch me and see. A ghost doesn't have flesh and bones as you can see that I have." As he said this, he showed them his hands and his feet.

And while for sheer joy they still didn't know what to believe and were bewildered, he said to them, "Do you have anything here to eat?" They offered him a piece of grilled fish, and he took it and ate it in front of them.

Then he said to them, "This is the message I gave you while I was still with you, that everything written about me in the Teaching of Moses and the Prophets and the Psalms is destined to come true." Then he prepared their minds to understand the Scriptures.

A god has flesh and bones and can eat fish and do whatever he wants. After a life lived totally as a human, experiencing all human emotions, Jesus is now and forever totally divine.

Ascension
(Luke 24:50-53)

Then he led them out as far as Bethany, and lifting up his hands he blessed them. And while he was blessing them, it so happened that he parted from them, and was carried up into the sky. And they paid homage to him and returned to Jerusalem full of joy, and were continually in the Temple blessing God.

It is very significant that the Gospel dedicated to Luke is the only one of the four canonical gospels that includes the ascension. Mark doesn't need it because Jesus-god is making his Triumphal Entry into Rome any day now. Matthew has the human Jesus saying good-bye (or hello) to his disciples in Galilee (which is a long way from Bethany and Jerusalem) and telling them that he will be with them always, right to the end of time. For this scribe, Jesus' ascension is the important sign of his newly-gained divinity.

Conclusion

The argument for a woman scribe for the Gospel dedicated to Luke rests in large part on the following:

A. The first-time introduction of six (6) named women:

1. Elizabeth, the mother of John the Baptist
2. Anna, the prophetess in Jerusalem
3. Joanna, the wife of Chuza, Herod's steward
4. Susanna
5-6. Mary and Martha, the sisters

Since the scribe of Luke is also the scribe of Acts, it is important to note that she named nine (9) women in that document as well.

B. Twelve (12) passages about women that were not in Mark or Matthew:

1. Story of Elizabeth and the birth of John the Baptist
2. Much expanded story of Mary and the birth of Jesus
3. Story of Anna, the prophetess
4. Story of the widow of Nain
5. Story of a woman anointing Jesus' feet
6. List of women with the male disciples
7. Story of Mary and Martha and Jesus' visit
8. Story of a woman healed on a Sabbath
9. Parable of a woman and one lost coin
10. Parable of a persistent widow
11. Jesus addressing women on his way to crucifixion
12. List of women at the resurrection

C. **Other original passages** showing gender bias:

1. Only conversation between two women (Mary and Elizabeth) recorded in the New Testament

2. "Womb" used seven (7) times out of nine (9) times total for entire New Testament

3. "Breasts" used four (4) times and nowhere else in New Testament

Conclusion

The essential elements of the theory presented in this book are:

1. **Paul's beliefs and** writings about Jesus form the theological basis for the Synoptic Gospels.

2. **The first gospel** was written in Rome (68-70 CE) and reflects the faith, hope and values of the Roman Church, consisting primarily of slaves. It was committed to paper by their scribe and dedicated to John Mark, Simon Peter's assistant.

3. **In Mark, Jesus** lived as a god and will return from heaven very soon to be inaugurated Emperor of the Empire of God on earth.

4. **The second gospel** was written in Alexandria (73-75 CE) and reflects the faith, knowledge and traditions of a Jewish-Egyptian community in a Greek culture. It was written by their scribe, using the Roman Gospel as a basis, and dedicated to Matthew, the disciple.

5. **In Matthew, Jesus** is completely human and is the new-and-improved Moses, teaching a new-and-improved Judaism as the way to the Kingdom of Heaven among the stars at the end of one's life or at the end of time.

6. **The third gospel** was written in Antioch (78-80 CE) and reflects the faith, sophistication and compassion of the Gentile Christian Church of that city. It is heavily influenced by Paul's theology. It is dedicated to Luke, a physician who accompanied and befriended Paul, and Paul is the hero of this church.

7. **In Luke, Jesus** was born human, lived and died human, but was resurrected as a god. It was this Jesus-god that Paul encountered on the road to Damascus, the story found in Acts, also written by the same scribe in the same church. They believed that the Kingdom of God was a present entity on earth and would continue eternally in the heavens.

8. **The scribe of** the Church of Antioch is a well-educated, highly intelligent poetess. The original material in this gospel makes a compelling case for female authorship.

9. **There is no** need for a theoretical "Q" sayings document since the scribe had access to both the Roman Gospel and the Alexandrian Gospel, and she adapted the material as much from one as she did from the other.

Most of the aspects of this theory have been written and discussed in academic circles for decades and some for centuries. Some of them are only now being introduced to the layperson by the media, like the Discovery and History channels, and groups like the Jesus Seminar. The laity is beginning to ask what else has been hidden by the academics (and the Church?) from non-academics besides the true role of Mary Magdalene and the authenticity of the Gospel of Judas and the Gospel of Philip and the Gospel of Thomas, etc. This book is written with the conviction that laypersons can decide for themselves what makes sense and what their faith should be. If three early Christian communities could disagree about the nature of Jesus, present day Christians should be afforded the same privilege. Let the debates begin!

When this material was presented to a large adult Sunday School class in a university town, the response was enthusiastic. The number one comment was that it was "thought-provoking." There were many who saw much validity in the theory and some who disagreed with some aspects. The two most disputed aspects were the denial of the existence of a "Q" document and the female authorship of Luke. One participant wrote that this theory helped him "understand why and how Matthew, Mark and Luke are different from each other, and how and why they are alike."

Intelligent church people have asked why three gospels telling essentially the same story were put in the New Testament. The differences between the three are rarely pointed out in church Bible study. We can speculate that each bishop of each of these three powerful early Christian churches understood the differences and saw to it that each gospel was included in the list of approved "books" of the New Testament. We can also speculate that since Athanasius, Bishop of Alexandria, wrote the final authoritative list of New Testament books in 367 CE, he put his church's gospel, Matthew, at the head of the list, even though he should have known that Mark was written first.

The last piece of speculation is that these gospels were written for the benefit of new people coming into their communities of faith, people like Theophilus of Antioch. They wanted the new converts to know the story of Jesus and experience the hope that the story raised in their hearts. There was no intention of broadcasting them throughout the empire, but they leaked out over time, and for that we can be eternally grateful.